UPPING THE ANTI

...a journal of theory and action...

number eight

WWW.UPPINGTHEANTI.ORG

★ Upping the Anti ★ Number Eight ★ May, 2009 ★ ISSN 1718-0872 ★

Layout & Design	Kelly Fritsch, Tom Keefer, and AK Thompson
Cover Art	Erik Ruin
Mailing Address	998 Bloor St. West, P.O. Box 10571, Toronto, Ontario, Canada, M6H 4H9
Email	uppingtheanti@gmail.com
Website	www.uppingtheanti.org

The editorial was written by and reflects the views of the editorial committee. Unless otherwise stated, articles express the opinions of their writers and not those of the advisory board or editorial committee. If you want to reprint articles or the complete text of the journal, please contact us.

Printed at Thistle Printing, Toronto, ON by Union Labour

® UNION ⬥ LABEL 6G

UPPING THE ANTI
...a journal of theory and action...

Editorial Committee

Erika Biddle, Aidan Conway, Kelly Fritsch, Tom Keefer,
Sharmeen Khan, Clare O'Connor, AK Thompson.

Advisory Board

Ernesto Aguilar, Houston, Texas; Kheya Bag, London, England; Dan Berger, Philadelphia; Honor Brabazon, London, England; Irina Ceric, Toronto; Nicole Cohen, Toronto; Chris Dixon, Sudbury; Bryan Doherty, Toronto; Caelie Frampton, Vancouver; Chris Harris, Toronto; Heather Hax, Toronto; Mandy Hiscocks, Guelph; Chris Hurl, Ottawa; Karl Kersplebedeb, Montreal; Alex Khasnabish, Halifax; Gary Kinsman, Sudbury; Krisztina Kun, Vancouver; Mike Leitold, Toronto; PJ Lilley, Vancouver; Tyler McCreary, Toronto; Erica Meiners, Chicago; Shourideh Molavi, Toronto; Angela Mooney, Ottawa; Garth Mullins, Vancouver; Scott Neigh, Sudbury; Jessica Peart, Vancouver; Ander Reszczynski-Negrazis, Toronto; Kim Smith, Edmonton; Emily van der Meulen, Toronto; Lesley Wood, Toronto.

Table of Contents

Introduction

The eighth issue of *Upping the Anti* took shape in the midst of a storm. Of our seven editors, five were on strike for 85 days between November and February with the membership of CUPE Local 3903 at York University in Toronto. Fighting precarious work and the neoliberal university, we weathered an unmovable administration before being legislated back to work by the provincial government. This exhilarating but exhausting mid-winter, three-month strike threatened to delay our production aims.

Nevertheless, as this issue came together, the editorial process revitalized our spirits, focused our goals and compelled us to publish something useful for future struggles. In our editorial, we engage with the challenges and opportunities that arise from the global economic crisis and the election of Barack Obama. Calling attention to the ways that politicians and economists are drawing on myth to reinvigorate capitalism, we consider the enduring question of hegemony. After evaluating some of the different orientations that today's radicals adopt when approaching this question, we outline how the left might use myths to help constitute a broader collective and radical "we."

As always, we begin this issue with letters from our readers. Heather Hax and etienne turpin revisit the question of catastrophe in their responses to our last editorial (UTA 7). Reflecting on our interview with sex worker and organizer Kara Gillies, Simone Skye highlights the importance of adopting a labour perspective on sex work. Melissa Elliot responds to Tom Keefer's article from last issue and offers a perspective on how non-native activists should relate to indigenous struggles. Finally, Greg Flemming responds to Neil Balan's review of Žižek's *Defense of Lost Causes* and Balan responds to Flemming.

In our interviews section, Aidan Conway talks with leading Marxist thinkers David McNally, Leo Panitch, and Sam Gindin about their perspectives on the current economic crisis. Long-time AIDS activist Gary Kinsman interviews Deborah Gould, a former ACT UP activist and author of the recently published *Moving Politics: Emotion and ACT UP's Fight Against AIDS*. In our final interview, Chris Dixon interviews Montreal-based organizer Helen Hudson as part of his ongoing project to record the experiences and insights of anti-authoritarian organizers in Canada and the US.

Long-time Ontario Coalition Against Poverty (OCAP) organizer John Clarke begins our articles section with an assessment of the challenges of anti-poverty organizing and movement building during the economic crisis. Next, anti-Israeli apartheid activist Shourideh Molavi assesses the terrain for Palestine solidarity organizing in the wake of Israel's attack on Gaza. Finally, solidarity activist Shiri Pasternak reports on the ongoing struggles of the Algonquins of Barriere Lake (ABL).

Our first roundtable discussion finds members of the Student Liberation Action Movement (SLAM) revisiting their organizing experiences in the 1990s at New York City's Hunter College. Our second roundtable explores the merits of study groups in radical left organizing and features participants from the LA Crew, Another Politics is Possible, the Activist Study Circles, and the New York Study Group.

Katy Rose begins our book reviews section with an investigation of *Asian Settler Colonialism* (U of Hawai'i Press), an edited collection in which authors explore the complicated colonial dynamics between "locals" and the native population of Hawai'i. Ernesto Aguilar reviews *Let Freedom Ring* (PM Press), an edited collection of political prisoner writing, and Frank Edgewick considers the long-awaited reprint of Semiotext(e)'s *Autonomia: Post-Political Politics*. Finally, DT Cochrane reviews Robert McChesney's *The Political Economy of Media* (Monthly Review Press).

This issue marks four years of *Upping the Anti*. We are pleased to welcome Erika Biddle to the editorial committee. We would like to thank former editor Nicole Cohen for her significant contributions to the journal and are pleased that she remains an active Advisory Board member.

Since 2005, we have published two journals each year, hosted public forums, and maintained an ongoing and improving web presence. We have done this with an all-volunteer collective of editors and advisory board members. Nevertheless, producing a journal is expensive and *Upping the Anti* is only made possible through your support. If you have not done so already, please consider subscribing to *Upping the Anti*. After all, nothing beats receiving mail! We are happy to announce that we now have a sustainer's program whereby you can make monthly donations to the journal to ensure that we are able to continue publishing. Visit us online to get a subscription or to make a donation. All donations go directly to the production of the journal. Visit us often at www.uppingtheanti.org and stay tuned for our website relaunch this summer. We look forward to your feedback on the new site's design and usability.

Upping the Anti number nine is scheduled to come out in October of 2009. If you are interested in contributing, please send a pitch to uppingtheanti@gmail.com. Pitches are due on or before May 30, 2009. The deadline for first drafts is July 5, 2009. For more information, please visit www.uppingtheanti.org.

We hope you enjoy this issue of *Upping the Anti* and we look forward to your letters, reviews, story ideas, and subscription requests.

In solidarity and struggle,

Erika Biddle, Aidan Conway, Kelly Fritsch, Tom Keefer,
Sharmeen Khan, Clare O'Connor, AK Thompson
Toronto, April 2009

[[[LETTERS]]]

Catastrophe and Actualization

Dear UTA,

I was pleased to read your editorial, "The Moment of Danger: Catastrophe and Actualization," in the last issue (UTA 7). "Crisis" under capitalism is certainly nothing new, as the editors point out. In this time of ecological and economic crisis, it is critical that anti-capitalists work rigorously to both make connections between the two and offer viable alternatives to the capitalist mode of production. You capture the essence of the problem quite well:

> If we are committed not only to an analysis of today's problems but to their resolution as well, we have to contemplate what forms of social labour would meet human needs (and allow for the historical development of human capacities) while – at the same time – working with a more intimate connection to the logic of nature's own contributions to the production process (41).

The journal's past work with anti tar-sands activists is a good start. I would very much like to see UTA dedicate a great deal more space not only to politics that stand against ecologically destructive production practices but to politics that point in the direction of creating new practices that, well, won't kill us.

For instance, while hardly radical, it is nonetheless important to track some of the new relationships that have been emerging between organized labour and environmental coalitions. Traditionally pitted against one another, organizers from both camps are starting to realize that the exploitative conditions that give rise to the commodification of workers are fundamentally linked to the logic of ecological exploitation. I admit to being seduced by the potential that these new relationships hold. However, we cannot fool ourselves into thinking that this coalitional shift will not bow to the gods of economic growth unless pushed to do otherwise.

Van Jones, author of *The Green Collar Economy: How One Solution Can Fix Our Two Biggest Problems* and an early agitator for labour and environmental justice coalitional politics, sees no way out of this moment of crisis without solutions organized by the private sector:

> There will surely be an important role for nonprofit, voluntary, cooperative, and community-based solutions... the reality is that we are entering an era during which our very survival will demand invention and innovation on a scale never before seen in the history of human civilization. Only the business community has the requisite skills, experience, and capital to meet that need. On that score, neither government nor the nonprofit and voluntary sectors can compete, not even remotely (86).

Unfortunately, this is the underlying philosophy that is currently driving the movement. It is incredibly important that UTA start to analyze organizations such as Green for All, The Blue-Green Alliance, and the Apollo Alliance, which operate under the umbrella of "green collar jobs" or the "green collar movement." These organizations seem to have a lot of traction with the Obama administration and are considered the vanguard of the new "green economy." I fear they are harnessing the lion's share of movement energy and potential but operate under the assumption that capitalism can be green or that the best strategy for intervention is to work within the structure available to us.

My concern is that Van Jones is right. As mentioned in the editorial, actualization of ecological production processes outside the sphere of capitalist accumulation tend to be limited to the agricultural sphere. If this remains the case, anti-capitalists are wasting their chance at organizing during a critical juncture, one that has the capacity to fundamentally change the way we live our lives. The environmental justice movement and anti-tar sands and anti-mountaintop removal activists offer the most convincing arguments against the logic of capitalist accumulation within the environmental movement. But, again, when most radical energy is spent blocking destructive practices without offering models of ecologically sound production practices, then Green for All and similar organizations will appear to be our only solution.

A critical eye to the green collar jobs movement is vital, but it is not enough. UTA can function as an important space in which to brainstorm ways North American activists can lend new voice to these critical debates and new direction to organizing energies. The open-ended conclusion of your editorial gives me hope that it will.

In Solidarity,
Heather Hax
Toronto, ON

Danger at Daybreak

Dear UTA,

UTA's most recent editorial (UTA 7) makes several points that deserve further elaboration, if only to underscore how important it is that activists and theorists engage with the tensions the editors highlight and confront the consequences they entail.

First, the editors are right to assert that, "The opportunity to confront the catastrophe directly – the opportunity to cut decisively against the narrative arc of progress – is forfeited the moment we lose sight of the fact that these events are not anomalies" (34-35). This forfeiture easily becomes a lethal foreclosure that undermines the possibility of any rigorous analysis of political economy.

Second, following Walter Benjamin, the editors contend that the "state of emergency" invoked by capitalism every time something broke down "was not the exception but the rule." With the current economic "crisis" now forming the political lens through which all other issues are framed, the importance of Benjamin's position cannot be overstated.

Third, as Benjamin argued and as the editors were correct to assert: "The unending chain of events is broken by a decisive moment of reckoning." This decisive moment is impossible without a dramatic rethinking of the myths of eco-vanguardism (eg, primitivism) and "free market" capitalism.

In addition to Benjamin's analysis, a return to questions raised by George Bataille (particularly in *The Accursed Share* and his earlier writings on expenditure) would have complimented the editors' position. First, Bataille forces us to confront the general economy that makes our restricted economy possible. That is, our present economic order and the presumed novelty of the crisis must be considered within a broader logic of energetic expenditure and its historical moment. As Bataille argues in "The Notion of Expenditure," "human life only rediscovers agitation on the scale of irreducile needs through the efforts of those who push the consequences as far as they will go. What remains of traditional modes of expenditure has become atrophied, and living sumptuary tumult has been lost in the unprecedented explosion of class struggle."

Second, and perhaps more important, is Bataille's analysis in "The Psychological Structure of Fascism." Reading this essay, it is possible to detect an analogy between the reduction of "heterogeneous" social elements to "homogenous" political imperatives in the first half of the 20th century and the reduction of heterostratic concerns in the fields of ecology and political economy into two divided and irreconcilable camps in the present. The ease with which these positions have become entrenched is indeed problematic because, as the editors rightly claim, human production has always involved the interaction between labour and nature (however broadly defined). Thus, the reduction that produces two irreconcilable approaches in current debates repeats an earlier fascistic leveling of heterogeneous social commitments.

Bataille's contributions notwithstanding, the most fitting adumbration of the current "catastrophe" comes from Benjamin's dear friend and comrade Bertolt Brecht. In Brecht's 1939 poem "The Parade of the Old New," it becomes clear that the question of novelty is outstripped by the rising fascist threat:

> Round about stood those who inspire terror, shouting: Here comes the New, it's all new, salute the New, be new like us! And those who heard, heard nothing but their shouts, but those who saw, saw certain people who were not shouting. / So the Old strode in disguised as the New, but it brought the New with it in its triumphal procession and presented it as the Old. [...] / And the procession moved through the night, but what they thought was the light of dawn was the light of fires in the sky. And the cry: Here comes the New, it's all new, salute the New, be new

like us would have been easier to hear if everything had not been drowned in the thunder of guns.

As UTA's editors make clear: whether old or new, the march of death will continue if our attention is not simultaneously oriented to the nature-labour relation and the radical transformation of the means of production this pairing demands. Only if our political struggles and theoretical inquiries engage with this problematic can we avoid the fatal error of mistaking fire in the sky for daybreak.

affectionately,
etienne turpin
Toronto

Sex Workers United

Dear UTA,
Congratulations to *Upping the Anti* for providing an excellent analysis of the issues facing sex workers in Canada and transnationally in "Sex Work and the State: An Interview with Kara Gillies" (UTA 7). Even though there is a constitutional challenge to prostitution-related offences in the Criminal Code currently underway, it appears that both popular media and academic interest in sex work has shifted to uncritical analyses of trafficking and sex tourism. This reflects, I believe, the ease with which anti-prostitution activists can deploy established narratives portraying racialized women in the Global South as victims in need of saving; an instance of a long and troubling history in South-North relations. The Western sex worker, while still portrayed as a victim, has become more resilient to portrayals as a hapless woman who lacks agency. As a consequence, focus has shifted away from the Canadian context (with exception for those identified as trafficked persons) during this critical moment when there is a legal challenge to the constitutionality of prostitution laws.

As Gillies points out, the hypocritical and contradictory role of Canadian prostitution laws is often misunderstood. Prostitution is legal in Canada. The implications of prostitution-related provisions of the Criminal Code are to de facto criminalize what is in fact a legal activity, with disastrous consequences for sex workers' safety. The criminal law prohibits sex workers from working in public places while at the same time prohibiting sex workers from working in private, indoor spaces where we are often much safer. The criminal law also makes it impossible for sex workers to access basic labour protections (such as employment contracts) despite the fact that income earned through prostitution is taxable. As noted by Gillies, as well as a number of academics and government committees, the different sections of the prostitution laws contradict one another. It is unclear whether the laws are supposed to be preventing the visibility of prostitution or preventing prostitution altogether.

Feminist research on prostitution has made a significant contribution by making visible the violence sex workers experience. However, the knowledge produced about sex work often obfuscates the complexity and nuances of the sex industry and the diverse experiences of sex workers. Gillies points out that only 5 percent of sex work in Toronto, and between 10 percent and 15 percent of sex work in Canada, is street-based. This fact is not reflected in the majority of Canadian anti-prostitution feminist research. Research about prostitution tends to make broad generalizations about experiences of working in the sex industry and the prevalence of violence workers face. Working conditions in different sectors of the sex industry in Canada vary greatly and presuming experiences are universal while implying that there is a total subjectivity of the "prostitute" is deeply problematic. This has resulted in the silencing (often by academics) of sex workers who are not considered to be "authentic" enough or who do not see their work as violence, and a "speaking on the behalf of" those who experience higher levels of vulnerability or insecurity.

The importance of adopting a labour perspective on sex work cannot be overstated, and this is as true for sex workers in the Global South as it is for workers in the Global North. Sex work, as Gillies notes, is understood by sex workers' rights organizations in the South as being one part of the solution to poverty many individuals experience as "underdeveloped" countries integrate into the global capitalist economy. Sex workers' labour is devalued and exploited through the same gendered, racial, and colonial hierarchies that are used to devalue labour in the global manufacturing or domestic service industries, and should not be conceptualized as exploitation that is somehow inherently different than exploitation in other industries. The only way for workers, including sex workers, to resist exploitation is through an understanding of their work as "real" work. Workers who do not understand what they do as work are unlikely to organize or to engage in political struggle to end exploitative and unsafe working conditions.

I believe that it is possible for sex workers to return from work safe and well, and that violence and exploitation are not any more inherent or "natural" to prostitution than they are to other forms of labour. The insights that a Marxist perspective provides for theorizing relationships between labour and capital should not be neglected as soon as the industry being discussed is the sex industry. I hope Gillies' interview encourages more people to understand the connections between sex work and other forms of work, and to become more aware of the complexity of issues facing sex workers in Canada and transnationally.

In solidarity,
Simone Skye
Sex worker and sex workers' rights activist, Toronto

The Struggle Continues

Dear UTA,
I would like to give a huge *Nia:wen Ko:wa* (thank you very much) to UTA for your continued attention to Six Nations' struggles post-Reclamation. As both a Six Nations, Haudenosaunee-Tuscarora youth activist and a university student, it is useful and inspiring to see discussions of our struggle in the pages of your journal. On top of that, to read such a focused article on our struggle, Tom Keefer's "Declaring the Exception: Direct Action, Six Nations & the Struggle in Brantford" (UTA 7), after the hype of Kahnestaton – the Reclamation site – faded away, is even more important. Other activists within various non-native organizations often ask,

"what's going on at Six Nations now?" "Is Six Nations still at the Reclamation site?" "I don't hear about you very much anymore," and so on. To be able to point people to your journal and to articles such as Keefer's is very helpful in my organizing.

I would like to elaborate on and add some of my personal observations, insights, and suggestions to the discussion raised in Keefer's article. To begin, the article gave a good overview of the current Six Nations struggle and the complex, unique dynamics that exist within it. The stress that Keefer placed on the need for solidarity between Six Nations and other non-native organizations and struggles is very much appreciated, as it is in fact critical to this struggle. However, there was one structural barrier to this solidarity that was not brought up explicitly in the article that I find crucial to point out: the effect of the continued marginalization and isolation of Indigenous issues.

It seems as though colonial powers have succeeded in marginalizing "Native issues" from dominant society to the extent that the left expects that *only* Native peoples are capable of being able to know, deal with, and engage with these issues. This is not something unique to Indigenous struggles as the same thing has happened to feminist, Black, Palestinian, labour, environmental, animal-rights, and other struggles. Our issues are separated, categorized, and marginalized as issues that need to be dealt with between "us" and "them," and dealt with case by case, and independent of each other. It is exactly this type of thinking and these types of approaches that prevent solidarity from occurring in a true, lasting, and valuable way.

I see this happening not only within dominant society but also within academic settings. Indigenous issues are reserved for Indigenous studies and other "race"-based classes while other courses that you think should include Indigenous issues such as Canadian politics, International Studies, and Women's Studies, for example, either brush-over or completely ignore them. This marginalization contributes to the alienation of Indigenous peoples within mainstream society while at the same time alienating non-native people from Indigenous peoples and our issues. In the end, we are left as divided and isolated peoples fighting huge issues on our own.

Furthermore, due to this marginalization there is a fear within non-native organizations and grassroots activists around engaging with Indigenous issues. For example, in a strategy meeting that recently occurred between various Native and non-native activists and organizations about 2010 Vancouver Olympics Resistance, a huge issue that kept coming up from the non-native activists was their "place" in this predominantly Indigenous struggle. They were scared that they would overstep their boundaries as "privileged" non-natives on an issue that, in their minds, should be Native-led. This fear led them to suggest that they should only work in a supportive role. This is problematic as it implies, in practice, that Native people are the only ones that should do the work in "their struggle." This view not only fails to see and treat our issues as two-sided *relationships*, but it also fails to acknowledge the power, privilege and responsibility non-native "Canadian" activists have in organizing within their own country and against their own governments.

The lesson to be learned from this incident is that non-native activists should not let their fear of privilege or lack of full knowledge of Native issues prevent them from taking on these issues and organizing around them within their own communities and organizations. We must recognize that this marginalization is not something we can just blame on the state or media or some other over-arching entity. To some extent we all think of these struggles as separate, distinct categories and see the differences before we understand the similarities. So perhaps this calls for a new type of revolution of the mind and the lens through which we see these various issues – a revolution undertaken by everyone.

A final point and suggestion I would like to bring up that was not fully addressed in the article is the danger of focusing only on the struggle aspect of our movement and missing the need to focus on internal, long-lasting alternatives to colonialism. While external struggles with developers, corporations, and the Canadian government are important and even crucial to our survival as a people, an internal social movement of unity, healing and cleaning-house is just as crucial an undertaking for our peoples. Too often this internal aspect of our movement is overlooked in the crossfire of protests, occupations, police stand-offs, negotiations, and legal proceedings. What this does is create a movement that is merely reactionary and places the power in the hands of the oppressor. Also, given that Haudenosaunee traditions provide men with the responsibility of the external realm while women have the responsibility for the internal realm, it automatically overlooks or downplays the role, insight, and contribution of Haudenosaunee women. Given the extremely traumatic history of our peoples, we need to focus on both the external and internal aspects of this movement in order to become the healed, unified, sovereign nation we strive to be.

This need is already being realized within Six Nations with numerous efforts currently underway. This includes the current restructuring of the Haudenosuanee Development Institute (HDI) that Keefer mentions in his article. What was once seen as an exclusive and unaccountable faction within our community is now willingly undergoing a restructuring process undertaken by our entire community. This is a huge step forward in unifying our community. As well, the Six Nations' youth movement, Young Onkwehonwe United (YOU), is trying to fulfil this internal need by organizing to unify and heal the nation through the gathering, inspiration and empowerment of youth. They have done this through such things as the 2008 Six Nations Youth Rally, their campaign to build a Six Nations Youth Centre, and organizing to gather Indigenous and non-indigenous youth for another youth-organized and run Six Nations Youth Rally in August 2009. As well, there has been a big push within Six Nations to hold clan meetings and return to other traditional Haudenosaunee practices for healing, unity, and long-lasting alternative solutions to colonialism. These initiatives offer much hope for the future of Six Nations' struggle and show how we would do well to focus equally on both external and internal organizing in order to achieve our goals for future generations.

Nia:wen Ko:wa again to UTA for support and continued commitment to our struggles, to Tom Keefer for your solidarity and all the hard work and writing you do, to all of you dedicated and inspiring activists out there who support and continue our interconnected and unified struggles, and to all of my relations.

In solidarity,
Ojisdari:yo, Melissa Elliott
Six Nations of the Grand River Territory

Risk and Responsibility

Dear UTA,
In his review of Žižek's *Defense of Lost Causes* (UTA 7) Balan makes some good observations. However, his comments sometimes do not go all the way and fail to convey the full weight of what Žižek says. In other cases, Balan goes too far and draws conclusions that Žižek would not.

It is with respect to Žižek's reference to "wagers" and "risks" that Balan does not go far enough. Here, Balan states that "ontology and politics are incommensurable but complementary." However, in Heidegger's "Nazi engagement," Žižek sees "the right step (albeit in the wrong direction)." This step is precisely the politicization of ontology. Žižek aligns Heidegger's "ontological difference" (the difference between "things" and the "essence" they all share) with Lacan's "Real" (the exclusion that founds an order). As is often the case, he gets there by showing how the divide that separates an existing order from itself makes that order possible.

Although this may sound abstract, it's a basic feature of all our activist experiences. For instance, CUPE 3903 – the union to which Balan and I both belong and which recently engaged in a three month strike – is not simply "itself"; it's split between being a union and being a wing of the state. Its existence is tied up with that of its adversary. This is where the "wager" comes in: it's not that ontology and politics are "complementary," but that there is no order that does not arise from the contingent "act" of the subject.

Here, "ontological difference" does not simply mean a divide between "things" and the "essence" they all share. Instead, "things" take on an "essence" through the imposition of the political subject. Returning to the union example, the union is split between the state and itself in its insistence that the financial support of the state is the solution to problems that arose in bargaining rather than recognizing the state as the problem's source.

As is perhaps well known, Žižek steals the "wager" from Pascal who believed that by giving up on worldly passions and believing in God one would gain infinitely. Before accepting the wager, people tend to want proof of God's existence so as to guarantee the outcome. However, it is only by taking the risk that one finds certainty. And so, while it appears in the beginning that both self and outcome are risked, in the end, the gain is certain, the loss is nil, and God's existence is proven. What Žižek takes from the "wager" is that certainty and order arise from what you have proved to unconsciously believe in the very act of doing it.

When Balan writes that "almost anything is possible if we are willing to accept the risk of failure," he misses this fundamental premise. It's less that one accepts failure and more that one produces a situation's unconscious truth through action. In "acting," (in Žižek's sense) one assumes responsibility for everything. This is the true "risk" of the wager; you lose everything you thought you had but gain a clean slate from which to engage in what Žižek calls "creative sublimation." This is precisely what didn't happen during the CUPE 3903 strike, and what disqualifies the strike as an "act." Instead of giving up on labour law and continuing the strike as a "wildcat," the union affirmed its belief in the legitimacy of the state by agreeing to abide by "back to work" legislation.

Balan doesn't go quite far enough with respect to "the possible" either. The point is not to believe that "almost anything is possible." Instead, it is to recognize that what becomes possible in revolutionary moments is exactly that which is not possible from the standpoint of the present. This is why Žižek adopts the slogan "politics is the art of the impossible." A true politics would completely change the liberal-democratic frame; the creations that might take its place cannot be known prior to their emergence.

Finally, there is a moment where Balan goes too far. He writes that "contrary to those preaching more action, Žižek's prescription highlights the need for finite planning and disciplined commitment to a concerted program." While Žižek's work might highlight this, there is a step that must come first. This step involves what he elsewhere calls "talk." This is because one can't have a "concerted program" without first devising the terms in which it can be understood. Without these terms, all action will tend to fall back into the framework of the (liberal-democratic) possible. Žižek's more fundamental contribution to political action is his insight that one must first break through the deadlocks of one's own position. For example, during the CUPE 3903 strike, the left was caught in the deadlocks of "vanguardism." It alternatively worried about telling people what to do or letting them make their own decisions – even if this meant accepting the legal frame of collective bargaining. We fell into the deadlocks of the 90 year old debate about "spontaneity" without finding a solution. In this sense, then, it might be surmised that a "Žižekian" thinking on the part of the left would itself have qualified as an "act."

In solidarity,
Greg Flemming
Toronto

Response to Flemming

Dear UTA,
Flemming's response is a welcome supplement to my review of *In Defense of Lost Causes* (UTA 7). That Flemming undertakes an analysis of the CUPE 3903 strike is notable because he demonstrates what to "do" with Žižek (albeit in a circuitous way): avoid some enforced, tight-fitting box around a political or material problem and avoid prescribing a proper "Žižekean" approach.

Let me address Flemming's specific points of criticism. First, on drawing conclusions that Žižek would not: so? While the review was a discussion of the book, it was also intended to encourage UTA readers to consider ways to overcome our present impasse.

Second, Flemming argues that I didn't go far enough in relation to Žižek's conception of "wagers" and "risks." Like Flemming, I acknowledge that Žižek develops the idea of risk and politics in ontological terms. The risk and wager of entering the "political" requires a movement into a place not covered by the safety of symbolic-social containers into which we activists, radicals, and self-hating fence-sitters regularly insert ourselves.

According to Flemming, "the true 'risk' of the wager" is that "you lose everything you thought you had but gain a clean slate from which to engage in what Žižek calls 'creative sublimation'." True, but I'm not sure he picks up on my point that the current situation is not dire enough for self-proclaimed radicals to lay it on the line. Take the CUPE 3903 strike. Certainly, opposing casualized flexploitative capitalism is important. However, I'm not sure that any "clean slate" is possible for those seeking guarantees for their careers, for reliable income, or for a stable site from which to call for intellectual, social, and economic emancipation. Bataille wrote about expenditure without returns. This is, I think, the fear of many with energy to burn: effort, risk, and utter failure. It would also qualify as an adequate political failure in Žižek's defense of lost causes. Recall the objective of the lost causes defended: the courage to endorse a state-form other than the current liberal-capitalist-parliamentary type with its biopolitical guarantees.

I agree that one needs to better consider the actual constitution of the risk-takers (not assuming some easy "We, together in solidarity") and the very nomination of "the current situation." At the same time, I agree with Žižek's advice about intellectual honesty. We must discard the safe cover available to those content to diagnose symptoms, repression, and drives that endlessly circle their object-targets.

Third, Flemming argues that I don't go far enough with the notion of "the possible" and that I go too far with respect to "disciplined commitment" and the "concerted program." For me, both of these criticisms are connected, if only because I'm inclined to answer them in relation to the explicit historical project Žižek discusses at the end of the book. Essentially, Žižek argues for a two-headed plan that plays between virtual risks and actual threats: anticipating the prospects of a political future where the left has little to no purchase or relevance; and taking measures here and now to avert the actualization of such a situation, thereby realizing something else entirely.

Flemming and I also agree on the matter of "talk." However, I argue that for Žižek, a plan and the good fundamentalism of indifference is altogether necessary. Idle, groundless, and dangerous talk may indeed provide a "pratico-pragmatic" opening. However, the spark that is unrealizable and impossible from "the standpoint of present" still requires some nomination about the timely necessity of an act. It is a responsive and rationalized move, even if it does bear fruit in the form of "creations that ... cannot be known prior to their own emergence." The premise: something needs to be done to mitigate the risk of the future being actualized. Ultimately, I agree with Žižek that we must invite and take terrifying risks now to confront a terrifying future-past that hurtles towards the present. For Žižek, emancipatory politics and radical egalitarianism are realized via the pure means of preemption.

Still safely covered,
Neil Balan
The east bank of Saskatoon

The Content and the Phrase

Myth and Hegemony Today

For the generation of radicals that grew up at the end of history, today's economic crisis comes as a relief. Despite the hardship the collapse of global markets is producing, it remains consoling that we'll never have to sit through another story about the inevitability of progress. And it's not just us: capitalists themselves have begun to break with the mantras that marked the neoliberal years. And while they have not yet been forced into contrition, many have at least succumbed to a new humility. This is because the future is all of a sudden (and once again) unwritten.

This change has been disorienting to everyone. It's worth remembering how, even at the beginning of this decade, it was possible for activists and other critics of capitalist depravity to identify with *Fight Club*'s Tyler Durden as he lamented being among the "middle children" of history. For a generation that viewed itself as having no Great War and no Great Depression, Durden's excesses – his sex, mischief, and immunity to commodity fetishism – were seen as a means of redeeming the quotidian by filling it with consolidating meaning: "Our Great War is a spiritual war, our Great Depression is our lives."

Less than two years after *Fight Club*'s release, America was bombing Afghanistan in a war that pundits promised would be without end. Less than ten years later, the global economy was in a precipitous state of decline. If the endless present of ten years ago was favourable to Durden's narcissism, then the abrupt end of that endless present was nothing less than a rude awakening.

In order to make sense of the wreckage, politicians, economists, and journalists have all trained their eyes on the past. All of a sudden, the Great Depression has become a serious topic of conversation. From *The Wall Street Journal* to *The Ottawa Citizen*, reporters are digging through the archives. Photos of bread lines and federal relief program work camps claw their way back into print alongside retrospective reportage on the crash of 1929. News websites scramble to run profiles of people who still remember the tragedy of the 1930s. Like ancient mariners, they tell harrowing stories that nevertheless all end with the same conclusion: *the story ends in survival, since I am here to tell you about it*. Considered as a general phenomenon, this return to history has been striking, and not least because it's resolutely at odds with the logic of late capitalism.

If our relationship to history prior to this crisis was one in which archival citations were stripped of their historic context and transposed into the register of style, this is far from true today. Historical citations are no longer marshaled primarily as a means of infusing commodities with affective weight. They now need to serve a much more basic function. This is because the market catastrophe has produced a situation in which unambiguous faith in capitalist progress has become impossible.

Slogans have been outstripped by events. "There is no alternative" has been supplanted by a desperate search for something that might serve as stabilizing ballast. Like the catechistic recitation of the lessons of Pearl Harbor that followed the attack on the World Trade Center, the economic meltdown has called up the ghosts of the Great Depression for one final curtain call.

■

A common feature of all these citations is that they seem to be pursued in the hope that the archive might be turned into a playbook. It's as if somewhere, in the details of the past, politicians and journalists expect to uncover a formula for resolving today's economic problems. Economic calculations are supplemented with religious mysticism. By identifying patterns in what are perceived to be the historic antecedents to the present, commentators have been reduced to reading tea leaves as they seek desperately to devise tactics to address the mess we're in.

On March 8, *The Financial Times* affirmed this practice by drawing upon the late American heterodox economist John

Kenneth Galbraith. According to the *Times*, "J.K. Galbraith wrote that 1929 stood alongside 1066, 1776, 1914, 1945 and 1989 in its importance. The world today was shaped by the efforts of governments to overcome the economic meltdown of the 1930s – and the consequences of their failures. Even if this economic crisis is not as bad as the Great Depression, it will have epoch-moulding consequences." The trick, then, is to revisit the failures of the past so that they are not repeated.

By responding in this way, these commentators highlight a profound but indeterminate connection between the moment of crisis and the revitalization of the ghosts of the past. For many people today, the necessity of learning from history appears to be obvious. From an early age, we are told that "those who do not learn from the past are destined to repeat it." On closer inspection, however, it becomes clear that "learning from the past" is not a self-evident process. Engagement with the archive is always an interpretive act. It is subject to processes of selection and emphasis that inevitably shape the lessons to be learned.

For this reason, the process of "learning from the past" currently being conducted by bourgeois journalists and politicians is precisely *the means* by which they shall condemn themselves to repeat it. If capitalism is presupposed as the framework through which the remnants of the past are interpreted, then capitalism will be the answer we receive. But these are not the only lessons the archive affords. It contains moments, objects, and recollections that simply don't fit into this framework. These irreconcilable elements have been inadvertently unsettled by the restless searching of those seeking to resuscitate capitalism; they are of vital importance to those who would like the story to end differently.

On this basis, we can see that there are at least two dominant orientations to history. The first orientation is favoured by those who try to locate the point at which they took a wrong turn. Once they find it, they can return to that point, correct their errors, and continue their predetermined trek on more stable footing. Following in the shadows are those who look for traces of an unrealized promise that continues to haunt them. For these searchers, the goal is not progress but actualization. How can the promise that continues to show its faint traces in the accumulated debris of past efforts be realized through action today?

Despite the uses to which they are being put, forays into the archive like the ones currently being carried out by journalists and politicians are seductive. Once their instrumental function has been served, these citations tend to point toward all that has yet to be realized. They produce contexts for collective identification. The interval between instrumentality and identification is the gate through which the generative myth passes into the world. It is the space of hegemonic action, the site of struggle for both capitalists and the radical left.

■

To get a sense of this process, it's useful to consider how, in deposing the feudal aristocracy, the bourgeoisie needed to draw on the strength of the nascent proletariat while simultaneously fighting against its demands from below. In order to achieve this complicated maneuver, the bourgeoisie gathered workers behind the banner of democracy and universal human rights. The promise of the banner coincided with a promise of an earlier pre-capitalist era buried deep in the recesses of their collective consciousness. In 17th century England, it was given vitality by being transposed into the eschatological register of the New Jerusalem. In 18th century France, the citation was different but the effect was the same. Nevertheless, the revolution carried out in the name of the Roman Republic gave way to the restoration of the Roman Empire with Bonaparte playing the part of Caesar.

In hindsight, it's easy to dismiss those who aligned themselves with a promise that could never be fulfilled in the terms through which it was expressed. For those of us who grew up at the end of history, the idea that an alliance could be formed on the basis of a promise seems downright naïve. Nevertheless, the citation of myth always carries within it the trace of its possible realization. The challenge is to find the form through which it can be fully expressed. Although the context in which it is cited limits the possibility of its realization, this does not mean that we should not orient to the promise it entails.

In *The Eighteenth Brumaire of Louis Bonaparte*, Marx proposed that, in bourgeois revolutions, "the phrase goes beyond the content." By this he meant that the stories the bourgeoisie recounted in order to accomplish its goals always exceeded the finite character of the accomplishments themselves. However, these finite goals would have been impossible to realize had it not been for the myths, the "phrases" that compelled people to act in the first place. The situation is not fundamentally different today. Like other bourgeois purveyors of myth, Barack Obama constituted a "we" by allowing those seduced by the promise of his citations of the past to line up behind a project that would never entail more than their superficial actualization. Between what this "we" will accomplish and the reasons they joined up lies a vast gulf. Obama will seek to paper over this divide. It is our task to blow it wide open.

Obama and his handlers have drawn deep from the archive of American myths to constitute a "we" capable of revitalizing capital. Nevertheless, the compulsion to identify with the promise Obama represents should not be dismissed as another expression of the mainstream's chronic shortsightedness. By actively drawing from the archive of unrealized American dreams, Obama revitalizes a collective longing for redemption. And while this longing will likely be channeled into projects that are antithetical to its realization, it is important to at least consider the possibility that, this time, we might find a way of turning the phrase that exceeds the content into a catalyst that can help produce a content that exceeds the phrase.

Activists have sensed this. Although Presidential inaugurations have often been important occasions for defiance and protest, Obama's term in office began differently. Instead of planning direct actions, some left intellectuals and activists – ranging from Noam Chomsky and Howard Zinn to members of this journal's advisory board – opted instead to issue "an open letter to those seeking to build a world from below, in which many worlds are possible." Although the call for action highlighted the need to be critical of Obama, it also pointed out that activists needed to "recognize both the historical meaning and power of this particular moment" and to reckon with the hope that Obama inspired. Failure to do so, the letter contended, would "ensure our own irrelevance."

> It is neither the time nor the place to critique hope or excitement on the part of people who have engaged in grassroots struggles in so many ways and won a substantial victory. The inauguration marks a watershed event in the often cruel history of these United States, and the whole world will be watching, hoping that we've done just a little to grapple with the legacy of slavery, lynching, segregation, displacement, and racism in general, both of the personal and institutional varieties.

However, while the letter points to the need to simultaneously be critical of Obama and identify with those who take him as a sign of hope, it remains unclear how this is to be practically achieved. It's obvious that hope is not in and of itself sufficient to transform the world. However, there is a danger that identifying with the hope of others while simultaneously trying to put forward alternative political content will end up appearing cynical and manipulative. Consequently, it's necessary to consider the connection between hope and revolutionary social change in greater detail.

To begin, it's useful to highlight the fact that people identify with the promise Obama represents because he has actively marshaled the most resonant myths of American history. The historical relay set in motion by his citations reaches deep into the past. It permeates every aspect of American life. The first and most often cited touchstone in this relay is the US civil rights movement. For many, Obama embodied the fulfillment of Martin Luther King's dream. But this dream also had antecedents. It drew deeply from the generative myth of liberal rights and freedoms, the myth of human equality as enshrined in the 1776 US Declaration of Independence: "We hold these truths to be self-evident, that all men are created equal."

Under capitalism, this myth – so powerful in its potential to mobilize people who desire to fulfill its promise – mainly serves to support the status quo. Almost from its inception, the revolutionary promise of the myth was channeled into the establishment of the bourgeois state. The myth's promise became decoupled from the revolutionary violence that animated it and became ensnared by the finite content of the ruling class. Nevertheless, the myth continues to resonate for vast numbers of people who are drawn to a promise that was never realized and never can be under capitalism.

By drawing upon the unrealized promise of the American Revolution, the unfinished Civil War, and the civil rights movement, Obama forged a hegemonic bloc within the US electorate. This bloc encompassed "progressives," Blacks, Latinos, the trade union movement, and students. Obama was also able to form clear cross-class alliances by bringing these groups into alignment with Silicon Valley capitalists and Wall Street financiers.

As commander-in-chief of the most powerful imperialist nation in the world, Obama is tending to ruling class interests. Nevertheless, under his direction, hope has become a force capable of stabilizing an order that was facing a serious legitimization crisis under George W. Bush. Through the course of his campaign, Obama thoroughly captured the aspirations of large numbers of working class people in the US by citing from the archive of past struggles. His identity as a Black man and his connections (however tenuous) to left-wing activism as a housing organizer in Chicago have only added to his credibility.

There's something real about the emotions Obama was able to evoke in the record-setting crowds that attended his campaign events, his victory speech in Chicago's Grant Park, and at his inauguration. He spoke directly to people about the possibility of thoroughgoing change and seemed – in his very person – to embody the promise of such a transformation. The genius of Obama's corporate backers is that they found a President who not only redeems America after eight years of George W. Bush but also relegitimates corporate rule using the veneer of progressivism.

■

Obama makes clear that the question of myth is bound up explicitly with the problem of hegemony. This relationship was a recurring theme for Marxists and other revolutionaries of the early 20th century who had to make sense of the fact that objective conditions did not automatically lead people to revolutionary conclusions. Thinkers like Georges Sorel, Leon Trotsky, and Antonio Gramsci tried to make sense of the disconnect between the objective and subjective factors underlying revolution.

In his *Reflections on Violence*, Sorel spoke explicitly about the role of myth in the cultivation of revolutionary capacities. According to Sorel, the function of myth was to orient the proletariat to the possibility of an indeterminate future that could be realized after a decisive break with the capitalist present. For the syndicalist movement, the name of this myth was the general strike. Although the myth itself did not have explicit content, it did stimulate identification with a promise that things could look radically different. Moreover, Sorel contended, it arose from and drew upon the lived experiences of the workers themselves. Consequently, Sorel believed that the promise of the general strike would return to mind every time the reality of the present became incommensurable with its promise. At its logical extreme, the myth pushed people to the point where the latent content of desire became identical to the manifest content of politics. In this way, myth paradoxically became the precondition for the production of new truths.

Developed slightly later, Trotsky's theory of transitional demands can be viewed as a programmatic attempt to address the same problem. Although the working class was objectively revolutionary, this did not mean that its struggles always led it to revolutionary conclusions. For this reason, Trotsky proposed that revolutionaries should articulate demands that would be intelligible to the workers movement (demands that accorded with those that arose spontaneously and without provocation) while simultaneously being unrealizable within the framework of the capitalist present. According to Trotsky, although workers would not gravitate spontaneously toward revolutionary demands, once they began to mobilize behind a demand that could not be attained without radical change, their desire to realize the demand would lead them into revolutionary action.

Both Sorel and Trotsky elaborated their positions to address the dynamics of 20th century capitalist development that made the terrain of revolutionary struggle very different from the one confronted by Marx. Although Marx could anticipate the trajectory of capitalist development, he did not live long enough to see the full extent to which capitalism would draw its own grave digger into the fold by using the trenches of civil society to diffuse and defuse concerted opposition. Because workers struggles in the 19th century were suppressed with strategies that had more to do with war than law, it was not difficult to believe that revolutionary politics could remain a contest between objectively divided enemies facing each other down across an unbridgeable chasm.

During the Russian revolution, revolutionary workers faced off against a crumbling feudal regime and a bourgeoisie that remained enfeebled in the backwaters of the industrial world system. Despite the difficulties the revolutionaries encountered when trying to constitute a "we" in Russia, they did not have to deal with the deep trenches of civil society. Their solution to the fragmentation of Russian life (a fragmentation that arose from the divisions between city and country and between those living in different cells within the prison house of nations) primarily took the form of organizational propositions. The party and its newspaper were the means by which the immediate experiences of everyday life could be transposed into the register of collective political intention.

These strategies continued to be important throughout the early 20th century. However, the objective differences between the situation in Russia and the one found in countries closer to the center of the industrial world system meant that revolutionaries needed to elaborate methods that addressed not only the objective dynamics of exploitation and resistance but the subjective dynamics of collective identification as well. Antonio Gramsci became centrally associated with this problem.

Like Sorel, Gramsci attempted to work out how the myth functioned within the emergent field of civil society. However, like Trotsky, he tried to operationalize those insights by transposing them into the programmatic register of the hegemonic "war of position." For Gramsci, if the exploitation, oppression, and disenchantment of life under capitalism did not automatically cause masses of people to commit to the struggle for a better world (and if the struggles that did occur often ended badly because they were pursued prematurely), then it was necessary to find a means of developing a tendency toward rupture in the very context and content of the present.

This meant engaging with the myths that animated civil society. Unlike Sorel and Trotsky, the goal was not to point to the promise of the moment of rupture or to cultivate identification with existing content but to push on and exploit the contradictions between the content and the phrase. By starting from the manifest content of the system and working slowly toward its latent promise, Gramsci envisioned the possibility of developing capacities and cultivating desires that would lead toward the decisive conflict, the "war of maneuver."

■

For Gramsci, hegemony meant constituting a "we" by aggregating disparate groups of people despite the fact that they may have divergent and even contradictory objective interests. Based on such a definition, it becomes clear that hegemony is an important category of ruling. Since capitalism presupposes contracts between free individuals, it has been necessary to devise means of preserving the impression of this objectively unrealizable premise. More instrumentally, the process of compelling workers to internalize and assimilate the logic of their own self-management made tremendous sense from the standpoint of good governance.

Because the objective contradictions within the aggregated "we" always threaten to overwhelm the prevailing order, maintaining hegemony is an active process and requires significant innovations on the part of the state and the capitalist class. Over the course of the 20th century these innovations enabled the development of a field of regimented action that now covers the entire planet and reaches deep inside each of us. Under conditions such as these, it has become self-evident to many activists that our objective should be to abolish hegemonic power altogether. This tendency is especially pronounced among those autonomous Marxists who have argued that the goal of revolutionary struggle is to elaborate forms of anti-power to decompose power itself. As compelling as these positions can sometimes seem, it's important to remember that – as far as Gramsci was concerned – it was not possible to envision a society shaped by struggle in which hegemony was not a decisive factor. The question, then, cannot be how to abolish hegemony. Instead, we must consider how to win it.

For Gramsci, winning hegemony involved engaging within the spaces and institutions of civil society. It meant identifying the generative myths within the hegemonic project of the bourgeoisie that had contradictory elements and that exceeded the content of the bourgeois world. These kinds of wars of position were not substitutes for the war of maneuver. They were its precondition. Their goal was to exhaust the possibilities of the myth's deferred realization so that those who were committed to it would come to push on the content directly and without illusion.

Accepting the fact that, in a context defined by bourgeois hegemony, the mass of the population would identify with the promise of its generative myths, the strategy of passive revolution called on radicals to start from the standpoint of bourgeois content and locate the latent promise that made people identify with it. For instance, to cite the most rudimentary example, in today's late capitalist culture, many people believe that they will share in a greater helping of human happiness by consuming commodities.

The customary radical answer to this behavior is to say that these people have succumbed to false consciousness and need to be reeducated or, alternately, to say that people should be able to consume what they think they need since only they can speak for themselves. What gets missed in responses such as these is that people's identification with the promise of the commodity is based on a real phenomenon. The commodity embodies both use value and exchange value. It denotes both alienation and its opposite. In the moment of its realization as use value, the commodity inevitably points to the promise of a production beyond the exploitative dimensions of labour under capitalism. Even if that promise can never be objectively realized under capitalism itself, it nevertheless calls people back to the commodity. Viewed in this way, the "consumer" becomes a neurotic symptom of the unrealized desire to become an unalienated producer.

If this is the case, then it is of little use to engage in moralizing. Although people can be made to feel guilty, it will not break them from the content that remains most closely tied to the phrase. In the absence of another alternative, even if people could produce an account of why they should live differently, they will be hard pressed to abandon their identification with bourgeois content.

The alternative, however, can be produced through the hegemonic action of movements themselves. If movements encouraged rather than discouraged identification with bourgeois content while simultaneously highlighting the promise it announces, then we could constitute a "we" on the basis of the promise itself. Next, we can demonstrate how the phrase exceeds the content. If we are able to preserve the continuity of the "we" through this phase, then we can move toward realizing the content's promise by emancipating it from its present condition by changing the conditions themselves.

This does not require that people have an anti-capitalist outlook at the beginning of the process. Nor does it require that the revolutionary add anything to what is already present in order to constitute a "we" capable of engaging in anti-capitalist work.

Following from Gramsci, we can conclude that the process of hegemonic war against constituted power involves three key steps. First, we must identify the myths that animate the present but that fail to generate an adequate content. These myths continue to resonate not because people believe they have been actualized but precisely because they do not. Second, we must recognize that people's resignation to the compensatory satisfactions of inadequate content does not mean that the promise of the phrase itself has been lost. It is therefore necessary that we learn to speak in the language of that desire so that we can encourage people to push for content that more adequately expresses the phrase itself. Finally, we must provide a concrete means of channeling the disappointment with inadequate content into revolutionary action aimed at emancipating the myth from its partial realization.

■

Needless to say, this isn't what the left does most of the time. Our use of myths is indeterminate. Consider, for instance, the predominant attributes of the radical left's "we." For most of the left, this "we" is informed by the habits of valorization. Often it entails a commitment to maintaining "who we are," of defining ourselves against the world even if it means that "we" are reduced to functional irrelevance. It neglects the most pressing problem that radicals might pose: what can we *become*? If we read this problem through Jean-Paul Sartre's archetypes of the rebel (who needs the hated world in order to constitute herself) and the revolutionary (who identifies with a promise of what the world can become and so embraces her own self-abolition), we can see that our movements more closely resemble the rebel. Consistent with this rebel orientation are a range of subtle practices that comprise the hegemony of the radical left's internal universe. At its logical extreme, it has meant that activist communities tend to become insular and exclusive subcultures.

It would be wrong to dismiss subcultures entirely. However, while subcultural spaces and counter-institutions have enabled important pedagogical experiments in self-realization, these experiments inevitably encounter at least two obstacles. The first is that counter-institutions, especially for those not directly involved in them, tend to find intelligibility as refutations of constituted power. This means that they (are thought to) negate what is by advancing an alternate content. For those not yet willing to choose this content, the counter-institution is, at best, a source of charming idiosyncrasy and is relegated to the margins it sometimes fetishizes. The second problem is that, when it does try to break out of that marginality, the counter-institution is put in the position of engaging in a war of position it has denounced. As such, it is unable to proceed on a stable footing. But if counter-institutions are in and of themselves insufficient to the challenges of the war of position, what is required?

■

The experience of the economic crisis and the Obama presidency should lead radicals to ask how we might constitute a hegemony of our own. However, to date, this question has not been broadly posed. Many of us continue to disavow the importance of hegemony. Others are willing to respond to the situation but not to take initiative. Still others are willing to consider the prospects of a left hegemony but fail to consider what this practically entails. Specifically, we have been silent on the question of how to aggregate social forces that currently don't orient toward a common interest in order to constitute a "we" capable of producing social effects that expand beyond the limited reach of the radical left.

It's encouraging to see that this discussion is (gradually) emerging. In early March, *The Nation* published a symposium anchored by Barbara Ehrenreich and Bill Fletcher's article "Rising to the Occasion: Reimagining Socialism." They write, "with both long-term biological and day-to-day economic survival in doubt, the only relevant question is: do we have a plan, people? ... Let's just put it right out on the table: *we* don't."

In order to address this problem, Ehrenreich and Fletcher invoke solidarity, "an antique notion until very recently," and point out that it "flickered into life again in the symbolism and energy of the Obama campaign." Organized solidarity, they conclude, is the central project for socialists today. Without disputing this conclusion, it seems crucial to highlight the limitations of the two-fold prescription of devising a plan and calling for solidarity. For starters, we must acknowledge that Obama channeled people's hope not simply by providing a coherent plan and calling for solidarity; he did it by cultivating a "we." The slogan "Yes we can!" became infectious.

As of yet, the socialist "we" to which Ehrenreich and Fletcher refer is not a functional grouping. It does not yet exist. Their argument falls short by failing to talk about the dynamic relationship between the need to devise a viable alternative and the need to constitute a subjective force capable of actualizing it. As Tariq Ali argued in his response to Ehrenreich and Fletcher, "until the emergence of a viable sociopolitical and economic alternative, *perceived by a majority as such*, there will be no final crisis of capitalism" (emphasis ours). Ali's note about the perception requirement – presented simultaneously as a precondition and an addendum – indicates that the project of constituting a "we" and the project of developing a plan cannot be separated.

■

In order to devise a plan, Ehrenreich and Fletcher emphasize the need for organization-based participatory democracy. However, they admit that "we don't even have a plan for the deliberative process that we know has to replace the anarchic madness of capitalism." But "deliberative process" presupposes the existence of a "we." The objective force required to introduce a new "plan" will have to be much bigger than today's self-identified radicals. And while material conditions will compel some to arrive at socialist conclusions, radicals will have to seriously consider strategies for bringing people together by subjective means if we are to maximize the potential of the new distrust of capitalism.

One of the most important contemporary examples of an anti-capitalist "we" being forged can be traced to the Bolivarian revolution in Venezuela. Whatever can be said of the limits of "Chavismo," it's indisputable that the Bolivarian revolution has inspired millions of Venezuelans to organize in revolutionary ways. Community councils, massive grassroots literacy and public health campaigns, and networks of armed "Bolivarian circles" are springing up to advance and defend the revolutionary process. Among the many significant features of this self-proclaimed "socialism of the 21st century" is the extent to which it has mobilized the productive myth of Simon Bolivar, the great liberator of Latin America. By calling for land reform, the abolition of slavery, and independence from Spain, Bolivar's 19th century campaign against Spanish colonialism was certainly progressive. But the myth (some might say the cult) of Bolivar has been used just as widely by Venezuelan dictators as it has been by the left. Nevertheless, Chavez and his supporters have taken possession of this national myth and created a hegemonic bloc within Venezuela and Latin America as a whole. With this bloc, they have pushed for socialist ideals and anti-imperialist policy. It's no less instructive to note that Cuban, Nicaraguan, and Mexican revolutionaries have similarly cited the mythical deeds of Marti, Sandino, and Zapata in their own projects of popular mobilization.

Despite these examples, it's difficult to imagine locating or mobilizing similar myths in the Canadian context. Unlike the mythical context in which Obama is operating, Canada did not have a bourgeois revolution that decisively broke the shackles that tied it to Britain. The closest that Canada ever came to a bourgeois revolution were the uprisings in Upper and Lower Canada. Bringing farmers and workers together with bourgeois leaders like William Lyon Mackenzie and Joseph Papineau, this movement sought "responsible government," free markets outside of British colonial preference, increased rights for Francophones, and control over the revenues of the colonial province. It was militarily defeated by better-armed and better-organized British troops.

As if this wasn't bad enough, Canada's very existence stood as a reaction to the successful revolution to the south. More than 40,000 defeated loyalists fled north and joined the sparsely populated British colony of approximately 150,000 inhabitants. The definitive claim that Canada is "not the United States" can thus be traced back to the very formation of the US republic. Despite the fact that contemporary anti-Americanism assumes a critical position toward American empire and global domination, Canadian anti-Americanism arose as a counter-revolutionary defense of the British Empire.

Nevertheless, the foundational myths of "Canadian identity" are closely bound up with our status as the "pacifistic," better informed, liberal cousins of the US. The power of these myths comes both from the historical experiences of Canada's domination by US capital and the resistance to that domination by the Canadian national bourgeoisie and popular left-wing forces.

The maturation of the Canadian bourgeoisie clearly played an important role in transforming the political content of Canadian nationalism. By the 1980s, Canadian capitalists sought greater integration into continental markets believing they could compete on a level playing field with US capital. As the national bourgeoisie abandoned the nationalism that enabled its rise, English Canadian social movements embraced the language of nationalism to oppose, among other things, continental free trade. One or another version of this myth also played a role in the Canadian anti-globalization and anti-war movements.

Despite this appropriation, the liberatory promise of Canadian nationalism is (at the very least) uncertain given the colonial nature of the Canadian state, its policies of genocide towards indigenous people, the historic oppression of the Québecois, and its long history of imperialist activity on the world stage.

It is therefore not surprising that the contemporary radical left has situated itself in opposition to the left nationalist leanings of groups like the Council of Canadians. Summarized in the slogan "No Borders, No Nations," this rejection of left nationalism helped clarify the movement's politics and radical identity. However, it did little to clarify how to relate to non-radicalized working-class people. Although anti-capitalist movements have generative myths of their own, they cannot be said to resonate with large sections of the population. They are rarely used to constitute a "we" that's broader than the already-active radical left itself.

Despite the difficulties posed by Canadian nationalism, it is not enough to deem myths inadmissible on the grounds that they arose in part from the preoccupations of oppressors. And while it's possible for resistance movements to draw from our own archives, this does not mean that we should be restricted to doing so. The mythology of a colonial project based on an equal and respectful partnership negotiated between settler and indigenous nations is central to the hegemonic construction of the Canadian state. As any school history text makes clear, Canada was based on something other than a ruthless and violent expropriation of land and resources. Yet this same myth has proven indispensable to indigenous people in struggle, and not simply in an instrumental way. The regular invocation of, for example, the symbol of the two-row wampum and its framework of peaceful dialogue and coexistence between peoples does not aim to valorize the Canadian conceit of a benign colonialism. Instead, it aims to highlight and leverage the gap between the appeal of the myth and the harsh realities of continuing colonial domination – between what might have been (or might still be) and what is – for liberatory purposes. The power of the myth lies precisely in its ability to mobilize people – indigenous as well as non-indigenous – to demand new content worthy of the phrase. The point is expressed in simple but powerful fashion in the slogan inscribed on the Algonquin blockade banner: "Keep Your Promise."

To get a broader sense of the uses to which the myths of the oppressors can be put, we can consider Jean-Paul Sartre and Frantz Fanon's account of the Algerian revolution. In his Introduction to *The Wretched of the Earth*, Sartre points out how people of colonized countries seized hold of the myth of universality underlying European racist humanism and turned it to their own advantage. The colonized "still spoke of our humanism," Sartre reports, "but only to reproach us with our inhumanity." The myth becomes useful precisely because it marks the distance between content and phrase.

For his part, Fanon points out that the youth of the colonized country, shaped by the nervous condition arising from the discrepancy between content and phrase, are quick to heap scorn upon the myths of their elders. Instead, they conjure up the memory of those fighters who resisted the initial occupation. However, even here, they do not seek to revitalize the past. Instead, the resonant myths that animate the anti-colonial project are transposed into a new internationalism. The political necessity of internationalism in the anti-colonial struggle leads resistance fighters to a concrete expression of the "humanism" they earlier reproached. "The barriers of blood and race prejudice are broken down on both sides," says Fanon. "In the same way, not every Negro or Moslem is issued automatically a hallmark of genuineness; and the gun or the knife is not inevitably reached for when a settler makes his appearance." Here, in the moment when the European bourgeoisie becomes the enemy of its own ideal, in the moment when the ideal itself begins to be realized through the anti-colonial rebellion, the myth is emancipated from the constraints of its content and becomes a concrete force in the production of something new.

■

As these examples make clear, the process of selecting resonant myths must necessarily involve experimentation. Luckily, we're used to experimenting. We do it whenever we introduce a new protest chant, campaign slogan, or banner image. Those that don't resonate fall by the wayside. In selecting unrealized myths from the bourgeois archive, we must assess our options based on their strategic value and not on what can most easily be absorbed by existing activist subcultures.

At its logical conclusion, cultivating a larger "we" by drawing upon the archive of generative myths demands that we break from the habit of valorizing these subcultures. Although they may be important and useful for our own purposes, activist subcultures will not allow us to build the mass-scale disappointment required to change this world decisively for the better. But while engagement with the problem of hegemony demands that we critique today's left, critique cannot be the extent of our work. After all, the purpose of critique is to realize the promise of the movement itself and to emancipate the promise of *our own phrases* from the partial realization of our current content.

In order to do so, we must begin by recognizing that the war of maneuver is doomed to fail if we don't also engage in a war of position. In this war, we must orient ourselves not toward that which we hope others will *come to desire* but rather toward the latent desires *already in play*. By orienting to these desires, it's possible to find deep wells of repressed energy that can be channeled into revolutionary activity. However, in order to tap into these reserves, we must start from the content in which they are trapped. ★

What they're saying about Canada's leanest, meanest news magazinists:

"Briarpatch speaks with a **courageous, discerning and persistent voice."**
CATHY HOLTSLANDER, BEYOND FACTORY FARMING COALITION

"I have much appreciated the **lively, irreverent, informative** insights in Briarpatch. It is just what is needed in a world of far too much dull and mindless conformism."
NOAM CHOMSKY

"Briarpatch is **solid, informative, and insightful.** It has no counterpart on the Canadian political landscape."
JUSTIN PODUR, ZNET

Briarpatch Magazine.
We march to the beat of a different drum.

Subscribe today at
www.briarpatchmagazine.com

[[[INTERVIEWS]]]

Contours of Crisis

Interviews with David McNally, Sam Gindin, and Leo Panitch

The current global crisis is likely to be the most serious seen since the 1930s. The immediate origins of the turmoil in "sub-prime" mortgage lending to the working poor in the United States, notably women and people of colour, are telling. They encapsulate key contradictions of contemporary capitalism and cut through the mirage of debt-fuelled working class integration in a context of sharply rising exploitation and inequality. By the end of this year, at least one in ten workers in developed countries will be without a job, affecting not only the livelihoods of people living in these countries but also those around the globe who are dependent on remittances from them. In the poor countries of the Global South, made vulnerable by growing integration into the circuits of international accumulation and the erosion of social protections during three decades of ruthless capitalist globalization, the worldwide downturn in aggravating what were already crisis conditions. In order to help get a handle on the crisis and its implications, Upping the Anti *conducted interviews on the subject with leading radical thinkers in Canada. David McNally is the author of a variety of works of Marxist theory and analysis, including* Another World Is Possible *(Arbeiter Ring, 2008). Sam Gindin and Leo Panitch have collaborated on numerous analyses of contemporary capitalism and the American imperial state, for example* Global Capitalism and American Empire *(Merlin Press, 2005) and are currently completing a major study on the subject. All three teach political economy at York University in Toronto. Aidan Conway conducted and edited these interviews in March, 2009.*

David McNally

Can the economic crisis that is unfolding be understood as a financial crisis – a product of the "paper" economy – or does it have deeper origins in the "real" economy of production, trade, and income distribution? How much sense does this distinction make?

One way of thinking about this is to ask why a financial crisis (which began, to be sure, in the US real estate market) has turned into a full blown economic slump, featuring the meltdown of manufacturing corporations. After all, the collapse of financial institutions in recent decades, such as the savings and loans crisis of the early 1980s, or the crash of the Long Term Capital Management hedge fund in 1998, did nothing of the sort. Financial crises trigger general economic slumps only when the underlying conditions of capitalist accumulation and profitability are fragile. And that was the case this time. In my view (developed at length in a forthcoming issue of *Historical Materialism*) global capitalism has been faced with deepening problems of over-capacity and declining profitability since the Asian Crisis of 1997. So, when the credit crisis started to unfold in August 2007, the world economy was highly vulnerable to any destabilizing shock that might emerge. But while a financial meltdown triggered the crisis, the latter has much deeper roots in the sphere of capitalist production, accumulation, and profitability.

As for the distinction between the "real" and the "paper" economies, a fair bit of caution is necessary. After all, the capitalist economy is inherently a monetary one – and this means that credit markets always play a crucial role. Buying, selling, lending, and borrowing are inherent in capitalist production and circulation.

Consequently, money and credit are entirely central to "real" processes of production and exchange. At the same time, it is important to distinguish actual assets (be they means of production or hoards of money) from what Marx calls "fictitious capital," such as stocks, bonds, mortgage-backed securities, and most derivatives. All of these fictitious capitals are claims to future wealth – wealth that may or may not ever materialize. In principle, fictitious capital allows an increase in the rate of accumulation by letting firms receive money today (which they can invest) in return for a share of future profits. But when paper claims on future profits become inflated beyond any reasonable prospects they become instruments of speculation that create asset bubbles. And in the run-up to this crisis we witnessed an extraordinary growth of paper claims to future wealth, claims that were clearly not sustainable. The result is the financial meltdown we have experienced now for more than a year. But I want to reiterate: this is not simply a financial crisis. It is a global crisis of profitability and over-accumulation tethered to a credit crisis.

Two final points on this. First, it is often said that finance has been a disciplining factor in the restructuring of capital in the neoliberal period. This is certainly true. But, contrary to quite a few claims, this does not mean that finance is "autonomous" of capital as a whole. Neoliberal wage compression (and the raising of the rate of exploitation of labour) would not have been possible without the whole gambit of processes that created lean production systems – retooling, computerizing and robotizing, shedding labour, breaking down older systems of shopfloor resistance, and so on. Finance aided and abetted these processes, but it did not create them. Moreover, these were global processes that involved the spatial reorganization of world manufacturing – and the enormous growth of manufacturing capacity in East Asia. It follows, secondly, that the crisis is not global simply because finance is international. The crisis is global also because manufacturing has become globalized in the neoliberal period as never before.

Even the mainstream financial press is diagnosing the end of the so-called "free market" experiment as governments of all stripes intervene massively in the market, dabble in bank nationalization, and embrace deficit-spending. How accurate is this assessment?

We miss the historical and social significance of this crisis if we do not recognize that key pillars of neoliberalism have collapsed – dogmatic free market ideology, gung-ho privatization of state assets, rhetorical (and sometimes real) pledges to avoid government deficits, professed hostility to Keynesian policies of fiscal stimulation by government (even if "military Keynesianism" was in fact practiced in the US much of the time). Now, as the state intervenes on a massive scale, there is a huge loss of credibility for the dominant ideology of the last 30 years – and the left should not underestimate the importance of this. There are ideological and political openings for the left the likes of which we have not seen in a very long time.

At the same time, neoliberalism was simply a set of ideological and policy prescriptions designed to restore capitalist profitability. If different policies are needed to preserve capital in a moment of crisis, then capitalists will readily embrace them. Moreover, other pillars of neoliberalism – the "law and order" agenda, the increase of police and "security" powers, crackdowns on migrant workers – not only remain entirely intact, but are generally being intensified in response to the crisis. So, this is a moment of real instability and uncertainty for the ruling class. It is abandoning key elements of neoliberalism and intensifying others. Classical neoliberalism is for the moment in shambles. But it is impossible to say what policy configuration will replace it, as this will largely be determined by the class and social struggles of the next few years. Capital will want a refashioned neoliberalism, a sort of post-neoliberalism. But social explosions of the sort we have seen in France, Greece, Iceland and parts of Latin America mean that it is by no means certain that they will get their way.

As for the state, it was always central to neoliberalism. Militarism, restrictive immigration policy, "free trade" agreements, exploitation of the Global South, anti-union laws, liberalization of finance, neoliberal education policy – all of this and more involved the use of harsh and intrusive state powers. But during this period the state was by and large allergic to nationalizing large chunks of the financial system and turning to massive stimulation of the economy. These are major shifts induced by the crisis. And, I repeat, they have opened up new ideological and policy debates – about the appropriate uses of public powers and resources – that were largely dormant in recent decades.

As the economic crisis deepens and spreads, references to the Great Depression of the 1930s have become commonplace. How far does this analogy take us?

To be sure, this is a profound systemic crisis of capitalism, as was the Great Depression. But historical analogies are generally more misleading than illuminating – and that is true in this case. To begin with, the overall weight of public expenditures in the major capitalist economies is much higher than in the 1930s. Secondly, operating without a gold standard (in any form) gives central banks today much greater monetary flexibility in responding to the crisis: they can dramatically increase the money supply without violating legislation involving ratios between currencies and gold. Thirdly, governments have responded with a much greater infusion of economic stimulus earlier on. As a result, the odds are that this slump will not be as deep as that of the 1930s; in particular, government spending should create a floor below which employment levels won't drop (though Spain could come close to 20 per cent unemployment this year). Having said that, this slump could be as protracted as the Great Depression, resembling in that regard the "lost decade" of the 1990s in Japan. And a long, drawn-out crisis gives the left a longer period in which to rebuild from its current weakened state.

The current economic crisis seems to be finally bearing out the analysis of many on the left that global capitalism and US hegemony never really recovered from their conjoined crises in the 1970s. From this perspective, disaster has been avoided thus far through the unsustainable expansion of massive pyramids of personal, corporate, and US government debt, increasingly funded by capital inflows from foreign sources. What does the current crisis tell us about US power and the international hierarchy of states?

To begin with, I don't believe global capitalism has been in crisis since the early 1970s. The evidence demonstrates, in my view, that there was a sustained neoliberal expansion from 1982 to 1997, centered particularly in East Asia. Wage repression, lean production, spatial reorganization, and industrial and financial restructuring raised the rate of exploitation of workers and underpinned a period of substantial growth. Over the past decade, that boom was increasingly reliant on massive debt creation, especially, but by no means exclusively, in the US. But credit expansion does not – and in my view could not – explain a quarter-century of capitalist growth. Only a genuine restructuring and recovery of profit rates could have done that. But the neoliberal expansion has now hit a wall. And recovery will not be easy.

As for US hegemony, the story is quite complex. On the one hand, there is no other state with the economic, military and political capacities to direct the global system. On the other hand, the US was not the key center of capitalist accumulation during the neoliberal era. East Asia was far and away the more dynamic economic space, and the huge stockpiles of foreign exchange assets in China, Japan, and South Korea reflect this. Furthermore, during the same era, European capital made considerable headway – though the crisis is creating counter-pressures – in terms of market integration and the creation of a common currency, the euro. As a result, I believe the US National Intelligence Council was right to suggest late last year that the world system is evolving in a more "multi-polar" direction. Yes, the US remains dominant. But its dominance is less sweeping than it was a decade ago – and will probably be less so again in another decade. Other regional powers will be able to exercise an influence that would not have been available to them in, say, the 1990s.

One key indicator of this is the growing pressure to diminish the role of the dollar as world money. The creation of the euro has already curtailed the dollar's global role. And China's call to dramatically increase the role of Special Drawing Rights through the IMF is an attempt to further constrain the dollar as world money. Both Russia and a UN panel support China on this, though making it happen in the short-term will be quite difficult. In the meantime, China is negotiating direct currency swaps with a number of countries – most recently with Argentina – which facilitates world trade without the use of the dollar. I believe that all of this points to a protracted process in which the US empire will confront increasing efforts to curtail its global dominance. There is no new center of global capitalist power that could simply replace the US. But there are also growing indications that the US will have less room for unilateral dominance.

A distinctive feature of the current financial crisis, in comparison with the recurrent episodes of financial turmoil over the last quarter century, appears to be that it has not been contained to countries in the periphery. What are the North-South dynamics emerging in this crisis and

what do they tell us about the organization of the global economy today?

Unlike any crisis of the neoliberal era, this one began in the capitalist core – first the US, then Europe. All previous crises of the neoliberal period – Mexico (1994), East Asia (1997), Russia (1998), Argentina (2000-1) were regionally contained. But this is a globalizing crisis that originated in the core. Of course, capital in the North will try to use tactics of "spatial displacement" to make people in the South bear the brunt. And this will increase human suffering in the most objectionable ways. Yet, so deep is the crisis in the banking sector that such tactics are not enough to stabilize the system. Most decisive, however, is the huge ideological defeat Washington has suffered with this crisis; its institutions and policies are seen as responsible for having dragged down the whole world economy. In this context, it will be much harder to impose austerity and structural adjustment in the South – by means of cutbacks to social spending, privatization and liberalization of banking – when the dominant nations are doing exactly the opposite.

I believe this is the most significant development in terms of North-South relations. Washington's crisis is likely to embolden popular movements and left reformist governments, like those in Venezuela, Ecuador, and Bolivia, to break with aspects of neoliberalism. Perhaps most significant in this regard, Ecuador has repudiated some of its foreign debts, claiming that they were fraudulently contracted. This is a most important move, and could open the door to further debt refusals – and perhaps popular movements to repudiate debt – at a time when Washington's moral authority has been battered.

More or less stagnant real wages for the vast majority in the rich countries have had as their counterpart (in addition to increased hours of work) steadily rising mortgage and consumer debt as households struggle to maintain relative levels of consumption and hope to share in the gains of asset price appreciation. To what extent does the current crisis signal the limits to this pattern of incorporation and social reproduction of subordinate classes? What does it suggest about the modes of resistance and struggle that are likely to have increased traction in this context?

It is certainly true that working class incorporation via debt has hit a wall, as people pay off debt ("de-leverage") rather than take on more. As a result, working class people in the North must now deal with living standards determined by their actual wages, not wages plus credit. This has big macroeconomic effects, since it means large drops in overall levels of spending and consumption. And for working class households it means real struggles to sustain living standards. In that sense, neoliberal illusions about prosperity through asset inflation (mainly via rising values for houses) are effectively dead. And that will have huge implications for politics. But, as I suggest below, how growing anger and resentment are translated into social and political action will depend enormously on the capacities of the left to respond in bold and creative ways.

Episodes of crisis would seem to offer important political openings to both the left and the right. The gathering struggle over how the crisis will be addressed promises both opportunities and dangers for the left. What are these opportunities and dangers, and how should we navigate them? What are the distinctive tasks of the radical left under these new conditions? What are the implications of the new terrain for left strategy, campaigns, organization, and alliance-formation?

A complex dialectic of danger and opportunity characterizes this moment. Obviously, the anger and fear generated by recession, job loss, and declining incomes can be channeled in quite different directions. Desperate, fearful people can often be pulled behind union concessions and national protectionism. And within protectionism lies the kernel of racism – the idea that "our" jobs are more important than those of others, and that "Canadians" need to protect themselves and "their" economy. Labour leaders who push campaigns like "Buy Canadian" or "Buy American" bear much of the responsibility for this. It is an especially easy – and dangerous – response by union leaders who are agreeing to plant closings and cutbacks to wages and benefits to "wrap themselves in the flag" as a way of diverting attention from real failures of strategic leadership. In so doing, they open the door to the scapegoating of immigrants and undocumented workers. Already, we have seen major moves against migrant workers in Canada, Australia, Britain, Spain, Thailand, and South Korea. So, if any left worth speaking of is going to be built in this period, it will have to be an intransigently anti-racist one that champions the rights of migrant workers and resists all forms of nationalism and protectionism. That is what makes the campaigns by groups like No One is Illegal so important.

At the same time, this crisis can create real traction for arguments from the left that creatively challenge capitalist bailouts while making the case for popular anti-poverty and anti-capitalist responses. Imagine, for instance, what might be achieved by radical forces significant enough to reframe the "bailout debate" by insisting that no public funds be given to auto companies without guaranteeing every job, preserving union contracts, and converting "excess" factories to green products (solar panels, or fuel-efficient diesel buses). Of course, such arguments would need to be linked to radical demands on behalf of the unorganized and the non-working poor – demands for free public transit, full rights for migrant workers, radically improved access to Employment Insurance, and so on. All of this means building a left capable of clearly, intelligibly, and radically posing alternatives that cut against the grain of the logic of capitalism. And it means developing these alternatives in a framework of anti-racism, internationalism, participatory democracy, and genuine non-sectarianism.

We can see elements of what is possible in this regard by looking at the mass social mobilizations that have swept Greece and France in recent months. In these cases we witness millions taking to the streets – in general strikes and mass demonstrations – against neoliberal responses to the crisis. In both countries, major new coalitions of the radical left have played important public roles. Without a doubt, the most important of these is the New Anti-capitalist Party (NPA) in France, launched earlier this year with 10,000 members. And, of course, all of this intersects with important discussions coming out of Latin America about developing a "socialism for the 21st century." So, while right-wing forces will undoubtedly try to intervene around this crisis, we should not underestimate the possibilities for building a new socialist left.

It would be naïve to pretend that we can artificially reproduce what has been achieved in France, where waves of mass anti-neoliberal protest since 1995 have had a material impact on the political culture. But it is clear that this is a moment in which non-sectarian forces of the radical left need to build new networks, new forms of collaboration, new common fronts for education and action in response to the crisis. Out of such initiatives, by creating new spaces of radical convergence, a new left might emerge – one capable of mobilizing much more substantial anti-capitalist forces in the face of this crisis.

Sam Gindin and Leo Panitch

The standard account of the current financial crisis attributes it to excessively risky lending by financial institutions. When combined with "securitization," which allows for the packaging and re-selling of income streams (e.g. mortgages) as financial assets, this reckless lending made it possible for the sub-prime mortgage market in the United States to act as trigger for a global credit crisis. Is this just a financial crisis or is it the product of other dynamics in the "real" economy?

Sam: This is clearly a crisis that started in finance, but you can't separate finance from the real economy. You can't understand it as simply a diversion from real accumulation or as a source of credit propping up the system. It has been fundamental to the making of global capitalism in the 1980s and 1990s. In this crisis we have seen how finance developed to the point where its dynamics and contradictions had a certain autonomy. It's a global crisis because of the way that finance has become global. But this crisis emerged in housing and mortgages, which are fundamental to the real economy, and this has given it a certain depth. You can't understand the depth of the crisis apart from the inequality that grew up over this period, and the way in which workers came to relate to the system in part as investors. However, the sub-prime mortgage market can't be understood simply in terms of workers wanting loans: it was the dynamics within finance, like leveraging and innovation, that made these loans possible. And the state encouraged it.

Leo: I would be willing to grant to those who see this as a stagnation or overaccumulation crisis that what they describe is basically true for a number of important industries. The auto sector is a good example. But we need to recognize that the last twenty-five years have been a very dynamic period of capitalist development in terms of technological change and the restructuring of industry, both regionally and in the labour process. So while it may be the case that certain industries were especially vulnerable to a crisis triggered in finance – and that's important to be aware of – this needs to be put in perspective. This isn't the same crisis that people were identifying in the 1970s. That crisis – which developed out of the strength of the working class and the contradictions of the welfare state, in conjunction with international competition – was resolved in no small part through the rise of finance, and this gave rise to new contradictions.

Sam: The role of finance in disciplining labour and promoting the restructuring of production has been fundamental. Even if you argue that finance creates no surplus, finance contributed to a larger surplus being generated through its role in disciplining and allocating capital across sectors and regions, so finance was functional to capital accumulation in that sense. In addition, when you think about the things that you need for an incredibly complicated and globalized capitalism to work, there's an expanded role for finance in providing different forms of insurance and services. Finance is speculative, but it is also functional, for instance in the areas of futures and options which provide credit for trade, or in the pressures created by the buying and selling of General Motors stock that have helped defeat the auto workers' union. Finance has also been central to American empire by fostering the penetration of American capital throughout the world and by fostering the flow of funds back into the United States which has been central to the US capacity to wage wars and fund foreign investment.

As states flirt with nationalizing large swathes of their banking sectors and intervene heavily in the market, even mainstream commentators are announcing the "death of an ideological god," in the words of Martin Wolf of the *Financial Times*. Are we witnessing the end of neoliberalism? Is the state back? Did it ever leave? What are the prospects for a post-neoliberal world emerging from this crisis?

Sam: Neoliberal ideology fostered the illusion that states were the problem for capitalism. But neoliberals have actually been very statist, even authoritarian, in all sorts of ways. We can see that neoliberalism was really about what the state could do to promote accumulation while ensuring that class strength was not built up from below in the process. The ruling class is incredibly pragmatic and they have been prepared all along to be interventionist if necessary. For example, there was very little criticism of the Bush deficits in elite circles, because a deficit based on military expenditures and tax cuts is not a problem from capital's perspective.

Leo: It was always astonishing how many serious people took neoliberal ideology at face value and thought the state's role was diminishing in a fundamental way. This ideology is now in tatters. Ironically, it suffers more on its own terms by saying that regulation was the problem. It becomes easy enough to argue that this disaster has been caused by the embrace of neoliberal deregulation, even if the truth is more complex. So at least at a superficial level, we are now free of the ideological stranglehold of neoliberalism. Even if you define neoliberalism more broadly as a form of social rule – a set of practices that rests less on ideology and more on how capitalism itself has evolved over the last thirty years – this form of social rule is in trouble. If the way that finance has been operating is in profound crisis, then it follows that a new set of practices and linkages will have to emerge if global capitalism is going to continue the way it did before.

Sam: It is difficult to imagine how the ruling class can say that what they are doing now is only temporary and that we're going to go back to the ways things worked before. At the same time, capitalism can keep chugging along without a lot of legitimacy because of people's continued dependence on the system and their fear of losing what little they have as subordinate class participants in it. For example, it is quite amazing to look at the auto industry and see that despite all the delegitimation that's gone on, the ruling class can still kick the shit out of auto workers, give money to Wall Street, and get away with it. US autoworkers are going to end up with their wages cut in half and will lose their health care at exactly the moment when you'd expect capital to have to be paying up. But there is a real opening and it could be very interesting.

Leo: The fascinating thing about the crisis of the 1970s is that it didn't interrupt globalization but accelerated it. It's an open question at the moment whether or not this crisis will interrupt global capitalism in a serious way, not necessarily in a socialist or even progressive direction, mind you. It's not clear that things can be put back together. Many of the states that are crucial to sustaining the project of global capitalism are fragile, and political fissures could emerge to prevent this crisis from being contained. There are real problems coming in Eastern Europe, and there are extremely reactionary forces in Western Europe as well. What Obama and company are most worried about is economic nationalism, which since 1945 has been seen as just as much of a danger by the American empire as the Communist threat.

The current economic crisis seems to be finally bearing out the analysis of many on the left that US hegemony is finally in serious trouble. From this perspective, disaster has been avoided thus far through the unsustainable expansion of massive pyramids of personal, corporate, and US government debt, increasingly funded by capital inflows from foreign sources. The apparent capacity of the US to sustain its position within these global imbalances as "consumer of last resort" has been viewed paradoxically as a symptom of both its weakness and enduring strength. What does this crisis suggest about the prospects of US power in the international hierarchy of states?

Sam: It is difficult to make any sense of recent events without emphasizing the imperial dimension of America's relationship to the rest of the world. The crisis began in the US, rapidly spread to other parts of the world and continues to be shaped by American political and economic developments. Defying the hopes and expectations of a great many commentators, the crisis has not produced any meaningful delinking from the US-centred global order. And in this respect the situation is dramatically different from the 1930s, when the world economy quickly fragmented. In the age of American empire, such autonomy is much harder to achieve. To be sure, the longer-term strength of American financial institutions remains to be seen, but the current crisis cannot be explained in terms of the external challenges to the financial power of the American state.

Leo: A crisis was predicted by a great many pundits on the premise that China and Japan, Middle East oil exporters, and 'emerging markets' with trade surpluses more generally were bound to stop their capital flows to the United States given the size of its trade deficit. But that crisis did not occur! Instead, it has really been instructive to see capitalists and governments everywhere that are responding to the crisis by searching for a safe haven turning to dollar debt, above all Treasury obligations. The Chinese call for the US to take measures to guarantee its "good credit" to ensure the "safety" of their holdings of US debt and even for a new IMF-sponsored international reserve currency independent of the dollar, need to be understood in light of what the head of the China Banking Regulatory Commission said in New York in February this year: "US Treasuries are the safe haven. For everyone, including China, it is the only option... we know the dollar is going to depreciate, so we hate you guys but there is nothing much we can do."

Even those European leaders like the German Finance Minister Peer Steinbrück, who opportunistically pronounced the end of American "financial superpower status" when the crisis erupted, soon started crediting the US Treasury for "acting not just in the US interests but also in the interests of other nations." The US was not being altruistic in doing this: not to do it would have risked a run on the dollar. But this is precisely the point. The American state cannot act in the interests of American capitalism without also reflecting the logic of American capital's integration with global capitalism both economically and politically. This is why it is always misleading to portray the American state as merely representing its "national interest" while ignoring the structural role it plays in the making and reproduction of global capitalism.

Sam: In this context, not too much should be made of such differences in approach as exist between European governments that favour more multilateral regulation and a US administration which stresses greater coordination of fiscal stimulus. Much more serious than the difficulties of keeping the Americans and Europeans on the same page is the question of how the crisis may aggravate the difficulties of fully integrating China within global capitalism. As we have suggested here, the danger posed to the US imperial role in global capitalism by Chinese investment in the US is not really the central problem. Rather, China's integration will depend on the US being able to penetrate further into the dynamics of East Asian economic development, to implant institutional forms that will ensure its compatibility with continued American imperial power. A new liberal multilateralism could afford the US, very likely backed by Europe, more influence over the parameters of Asian economic development.

If and when, during the next decades, the foundations of American empire were really to crumble, class struggles within the imperial heartland itself would likely play a major role in bringing this on – precisely because of the way in which the external and internal dimensions of American empire are intertwined. At the same time, the ability to pacify the citizens of the empire is critically dependent on the ability to maintain wider structures of global exploitation and integration. Making apparent the linkages between these different sources of oppression is therefore more pressing than ever. But just as the re-regulation agenda may tend to take the wind out of the sails of domestic opposition, so proposals for the return to a more cooperative, multilateral international order may tend to prematurely harmonize the contradictions generated by global power structures. The progressive transformation of the economic world order requires the kind of international solidarity that advances struggles within each state, not multilateralism among states as they are presently constituted.

As the economic crisis deepens, references to the Great Depression of the 1930s have become commonplace. What are the similarities and differences between the crisis and responses to it in the 1930s and today?

Sam: We've been thinking about this by looking at when people began to rebel in the 1930s. You don't really see much resistance until about 1932. So it was a good three years before the big marches of the unemployed in Detroit, for example. And it's not until 1933 or 1934 that the sustained efforts at organizing got going. People were really shocked and numbed. What's interesting is that around 1934 there was a real economic upturn. Unemployment only drops to 17 percent from 25 percent, but you have economic growth rates of 20-25 percent for two or three years before the second recession. It was only really when the economy started to improve that people had the confidence to begin to fight back. After the second collapse in 1937, the United Auto Workers union was almost completely destroyed at General Motors. In Canada, the union survived by setting up bowling leagues and rod and gun clubs. They had almost no base in the plants then, and that didn't really change until the war.

Leo: Most people on the left think that state intervention and re-regulation is where we ought to go. This is limited and naïve.

If you look at the 1930s, what happened is that the state stepped in and saved financial capital as a fraction of the capitalist class, and then nurtured it back to health for thirty years. It would be a tragedy if the outcome of this crisis were a re-regulation that merely saved capitalism again. It's misleading to think that the state as it is presently constructed is going to intervene in ways that serve left objectives. What are needed are the kinds of reforms that could be built on as part of a process of more fundamental change. Socialists didn't think enough about this is the 1930s and 1940s. Many of those reforms were good and necessary, but they involved a bureaucratic capitalist state, distant from the working class, introducing reforms of a kind that didn't lay any basis for moving forward in a more radical way. Now, you're not going to get anywhere as a socialist without offering and fighting for immediate reforms (you can't say "wait for the revolution"), but the danger is that in the process you promote, as in some ways was done in the wake of the Great Depression, reforms that will meet certain needs but won't help lay the basis for moving beyond the system.

Sam: If we look at the Great Depression in a broader historical perspective, a few other things stand out. From World War I on, the working class emerged as a democratic force. This created problems in an international monetary system based on the Gold Standard, which was supposed to lead to automatic adjustments. But you now had workers who would not accept that kind of devastating discipline and adjustment. So a conflict emerged between workers and finance, and the question was how to resolve it. With World War I, the Bretton Woods system, and the growth of welfare states, you get one kind of resolution, which worked for a time but gave rise to contradictions and was ultimately unsustainable. Out of its crisis in the 1970s, we ended up with liberal finance once again smashing workers, and this is now in crisis. So there is a question about where things can go from here.

More or less stagnant real wages for the vast majority in the rich countries have had as their counterpart (in addition to increased hours of work) steadily rising debt levels as households struggle to maintain relative levels of consumption and hope to share in the gains from asset inflation. To what extent does the current crisis signal the limits to this pattern of incorporation and social reproduction of subordinate classes?

Sam: This question has to be understood against the backdrop of the discipline that finance was able to exert on industries to promote restructuring in such a way that workers were more disciplined, were working at a higher rate of exploitation, while at the same time limiting wage increases. Workers were not able to sustain (especially in the last decade) their relative standards of living without getting in over their heads in terms of mortgage debt and other forms of consumer credit. The way whole working class families had increased their hours of work to sustain their standard of living reached a limit by the end of the 1990s. While the structure of consumer credit dependence was in place by the 1950s, and especially the 1970s, it really accelerated in the last decade, especially around mortgage debt.

Leo: The new industries that emerged in this period of restructuring didn't produce as many stable well-paying working class jobs with benefits as the old sectors had. They might have done so for a number of computer programmers and technicians, but not for large numbers of workers. That's not to say that these industries weren't profitable and accumulating in a very dynamic way, but the relative dearth of decent jobs did produce realization problems, and credit played a role in bridging this gap for a time. But this pattern of integration is now in crisis.

What are these opportunities and dangers that are emerging over responses to the crisis, and how should we navigate them? What are the distinctive tasks of the radical left under these new conditions?

Leo: Because of the role of finance, this crisis may lead people on the left to look for an alliance pitting workers and industrial capital against rentiers. Since Henry George in the 19th century this has been the most common form of working class politics. The default politics has not been revolutionary, but has rather been about looking towards an alliance with a rooted national or regional capitalist class. Of course it has been some time since national capital has been interested in this kind of alliance. They may be more inclined towards this in some form today, and if that's true, then progressives are likely to head in that direction, to the detriment of working for more fundamental change.

Sam: In terms of resistance and struggle, there is no reason to have confidence in spontaneous developments. There will be acts of resistance, to be sure, but we shouldn't expect this to become generalized. People are reacting in completely confused ways, for example by attacking the rich, but also attacking Chinese workers or domestic auto workers. However, there is a real opening because so many people have exhausted their capacity to survive in what had become the normal ways – more hours worked, debt, etc. Larger questions have to be raised immediately. More radical responses, like nationalizations, have to be talked about now. That's the only way these things ever get on the agenda. And they have to be linked to the immediate struggles and demands that will emerge as people try to defend themselves.

In the auto industry, for example, as long as the union is content to say "we are not the problem," it goes nowhere. The discussion then becomes about how much you're going to give up. The only way the union could have survived this would have been to act in a much bolder way by refusing to even discuss further concessions and by trying to provoke a larger discussion. In the United States, auto workers should have put healthcare on the agenda a long time ago, even if it meant a strike where they would be attacked at first. This would have given them the chance to defend themselves by standing up for everyone else. This is now going to happen with pensions in Canada.

Something like 500 auto parts plants will be closing in the United States over the next couple of years. For many workers and communities that's all they have. If people would take plants over, that would be a way to get the debate going. We need to start a discussion about the plants that have closed, even before the crisis, and how they could be re-opened and converted for new kinds of green production. Of course, to do this requires a plan, so it immediately raises the question of democratic planning at the community level. Windsor, in Ontario, already had a crisis before the crisis, so public debate needs to be sparked about how to prevent Windsor from becoming another Detroit, for example. You have to try to change the agenda in a way that allows you to fight and mobilize. This would also get the union talking to its unemployed members, which they're not doing apart from some job-training programs. These people are not being mobilized at all.

Leo: To even imagine this, unions have to be non-corporatist and they have to be willing to attack the companies. You have to talk about communities and their productive capacities, not just the companies. To do this requires confidence, vision, and internal democracy. The lack of democracy is a big part of why the union is incapable of taking this kind of thing on. What the union has become very good at doing is controlling internal dissent. The problem is partly the very nature of unions. Marx himself seemed to be of two minds about this. Sometimes he described unions as "schools for socialism," and sometime he had very critical things to say about the role they played. You can take a union so far but it organizes people for reasons other than radical social change; it is a bit like an insurance company. Now, one wishes that you had the kind of union leaderships that in the old days were prepared to join, and encourage as many of their members as possible to join, labour parties, the Industrial Workers of the World, Communist parties, etc., but these kinds of leaders are few and far between today.

Sam: There's a limit to what you can expect from unions, and I think the situation they're in now makes it very difficult to imagine them playing a leading role. But there is an opportunity for the radical left, because a significant number of union members and those who have lost their jobs will be frustrated by the broken promises, or the limits of winning of a few extra weeks of unemployment insurance. Of course this demand is important, but this crisis is of such a kind that this is a band-aid measure. That's the main reform that's being advanced by unions.

There are two ways to go for the radical left in the short term. One is to get street mobilization going and to take more radical action within the unemployment insurance demand, for example by occupying unemployment offices. Another is to fight to expand the demands: why should it just be about unemployment insurance, why not dental care and pharmacare, why not public housing, and so on? Instead of just talking about the stimulus plan and its size, we should talk about democratizing the process: what are we stimulating? New forms of working-class organization need to emerge in this crisis, and a good place to start is at the community, or city-wide, level. Thinking a bit longer term, a great many non-traditional workers are going to be facing intense pressures and can be mobilized and turned to radical politics. They can play a role in building the kinds of socialist formations that unions can't be. It seems clear that this is what we have to be working towards. Clearly, you need to have parties that are both inside and outside unions.

The radical left needs to be in the public eye and, for lack of a better term, "sound crazy." We need to raise big questions and demands even if we're not sure of whether or not they will work. We need to shift the terms of debate from "bailouts" to saving the infrastructure and skills of communities and converting them to new socially useful forms of green production. If we take the environmental question seriously, then every factory that produces anything is going to have to make some major transitions. It's not just about energy-saving, it's about making the things that are going to be necessary for a broader shift in what we produce and consume: wind turbines, materials needed for retrofitting, etc. The list is incredibly long once you start thinking about it. Communities are going to need to overhaul a lot of infrastructure in coming years. Without a broader democratic plan that makes this about something other than bringing new products to the market, this risks amounting to providing subsidies to a new environmental-industrial complex. We have to raise the bigger questions about democratic planning.

Leo: We need to raise the question of nationalizations, but in a different way from the old Communist Party approach: we need to insist that nationalization involve democratizing the state, because people are rightfully fearful of the state. When you talk about nationalizing the banks, for example, people are often skeptical, and for some good reasons. Broadening the discussion in this way also provides for some common ground with the people that came up in the anti-globalization movement who, rightfully but also in some limiting ways, have been very anti-statist and very concerned with the question of democracy. So things have to be approached in terms of democratization.

Ultimately, this is still going to involve trying to get people into a broad socialist formation with an agenda that is not limited to producing literature and protesting, but is oriented to getting people involved in and excited about developing a radical plan for Canada, in solidarity with similar projects internationally. ★

AIDS Activism and the Politics of Emotion

An Interview with Deborah Gould

Deborah Gould is an activist, researcher and professor in Women's Studies and Sociology at the University of Pittsburgh. She is the author of Moving Politics: Emotion and ACT UP's Fight Against AIDS, *University of Chicago Press, 2009. Her main intellectual interests are political emotion and contentious politics. She was a member of ACT UP/Chicago for many years as well as Queer to the Left, where she primarily worked on issues of low-cost housing and gentrification. She is a founding member of the art/ activist/research group Feel Tank Chicago, and is most inspired these days by the alternative globalization movement in all of its local manifestations. Deborah Gould was interviewed by Gary Kinsman in February 2009. Gary Kinsman was involved in the AIDS Activism of AIDS ACTION NOW! in Toronto in the late 1980s and early 1990s.*

Perhaps we can start with your activism. Can you tell us a bit about your involvement in ACT UP/Chicago and in Queer to the Left?

I got involved in ACT UP/Chicago in 1989 and it quickly became my life. It was utterly compelling to me politically, sexually, intellectually, emotionally, imaginatively. I wasn't consciously aware of this at the time, but in retrospect I think what kept me there, in addition to fighting AIDS, was that ACT UP felt to me like a place where I could learn and grow, become politicized and radicalized, and try out new ways of thinking, feeling, and being in the world with a bunch of really exciting people. I dropped out of graduate school a year after getting involved, in part because I was learning so much more from being in the movement, but also because ACT UP felt so vital in terms of the political work we were doing, the enormous stakes involved, the friendships, the intimacies, the queerness, the collectivity, the sense of possibility. It was a tremendously important time in my life, so much so that I divide my life into before and after ACT UP. When it ended in January 1995 I went into a depression. I think a lot of us did.

In 1996 or so, some of the dykes from ACT UP got together with other queer women and formed a group named something like "Ad Hoc Group of Dykes." We were trying to figure out what we wanted to be doing politically. One of our projects was a broadside "It's Time To End The Gay Rights Movement As We Know It" (published in Spring 1997; available at www.queertotheleft.org). It was mostly a critique of the growing conservatism in the mainstream lesbian and gay movement as issues like gays in the military and gay marriage took over the agenda. It was also an attempt to put forward a vision of a queer leftist politic. Queer to the Left grew out of that formation, but this time with queers of all genders. Queer to the Left continued the work of challenging the politics of the more establishment-oriented lesbian and gay movement, but what most excited me was the work we did on the death penalty, police brutality, and issues of low-cost housing and gentrification. Gay activism at that time seemed to be absorbed in lobbying, endorsing candidates and electoral politics, and none of us were moved by any of that. Queer to the Left provided a route for other sorts of queer political desires. Our goal was to investigate and illuminate the ways in which homophobia and heterosexism intersect with racial and economic oppression, and to build a politic out of that analysis. People who slam identity politics for not being concerned about class fail to understand the diversity of politics among those who organize along identity lines. In our case, we strongly identified as queers in the LGBT sense of the term and in the anti-normative sense too, but our political desires, while informed by being queer, encompassed sexual liberation and a lot more. That kind of messiness seems to be lost on those who criticize identity politics.

Something really important that I learned from my comrades in Queer to the Left was about the politics of public space and the value of urban street life, where different sorts of people come into relation with one another, thereby opening up different sorts of possibilities, collectivities, solidarities, and practices. That was a big part of our politic and something that energized me a great deal. Queer to the Left was active until 2004 or 2005.

Another group you've been involved in is Feel Tank Chicago. What is Feel Tank?

Feel Tank Chicago was formed in 2001 or 2002. We are a collaborative group of activists, artists, and academics interested in political emotion, in the ways that feelings are shaped by, play out in and influence "the political." We've been particularly interested in political depression and despair, feelings that we ourselves experience and that we believe circulate widely in the US social landscape. We see these bad feelings not as indications of political apathy or indifference but instead as affective states that indicate desire for a different world, one where our needs and wants would be taken seriously, where people would want to engage with the political because it would be a site for real participatory decision-making about the central issues shaping our lives. Feel Tank's "Parades of the Politically Depressed" have been attempts to collectivize and politicize our bad feelings and to plumb the political potential of a camaraderie based on political depression.

Can you tell us about your new book, *Moving Politics: Emotion and ACT UP's Fight Against AIDS*?

Moving Politics is a history of AIDS activism in the US – with a special focus on ACT UP – and an exploration of the affective stimuli and blockages to political activism. Themes that I take up in the book include ambivalence and activism; events and their emotional effects; the emotion work of social movements; movements as sites of collective world-making; the erotics, humour and intensities of activism; the seduction of moderation; solidarity and its fracturing; and political despair.

My interest in political emotion is tied to the question of political imaginaries and their conditions of possibility: how do people come to their understandings of the world and their sense of what else might be possible? How are attitudes about what is politically possible or desirable generated, reproduced over time and sometimes transformed, and with what sorts of political effects?

Consider the case of AIDS activism. It was never inevitable that lesbians, gay men, and other sexual and gender outlaws would become politically active in the face of AIDS. So, why did they turn toward activism rather than disassociating from the crisis altogether? Why did early AIDS activism take the forms it did, marked by care-taking and service provision, vigils and lobbying? Why in the late 1980s did thousands dramatically shift course and defiantly take to the streets after more than a decade of routine interest-group politics? Given the mainstream gay community's rejection of militancy in the mid-1970s, how was a direct-action group like ACT UP able to garner widespread community support for so many years? And why did ACT UP decline in the early 1990s even as the AIDS epidemic continued unabated? Those questions pointed me toward shifts in the political horizon within lesbian and gay communities, and it quickly became apparent to me that understanding those shifts required exploring political feelings, their sources, how they take hold and circulate, how they are altered and the role they play in shaping senses of political (im)possibility.

In this case, a structure of ambivalence in lesbian and gay communities strongly shaped collective political responses to the AIDS crisis. This widely circulating, contradictory constellation of positive and negative affective states, simultaneous self-love and self-doubt, gay pride and gay shame, attraction to and repulsion from dominant society, derives from living in a heteronormative society. This structure of ambivalence, and lesbians' and gay men's navigations of it, has significant political effects, in any given moment helping to shape attitudes about what is politically possible, desirable and necessary, thus influencing whether and how activism is undertaken.

In the earliest years of the AIDS crisis, which were years of immense fear and grief, lesbians and gay men created organizations to care for the sick and dying, lobbied, and held candlelit vigils to draw attention to the crisis. Gay pride was an important factor motivating these responses. As I sorted through lesbian and gay newspapers from that period, I found that other feeling states were in play as well, especially gay shame and a corollary fear of intensified social rejection, and they too helped to establish, and delimit, the political horizon in those early years. Those more negative affective states pervaded gay public discourse. I argue that they encouraged AIDS advocates and activists to pursue reputable forms of activism (like service provision, lobbying, and vigils) and discouraged anything that might rock the boat too much. So the specific configuration of lesbian and gay ambivalence in that moment opened up some political possibilities and foreclosed others. Obviously, this emotional and imaginative terrain had to shift in order for ACT UP to emerge. My book explores that shift, then turns to the question of the movement's development and sustainability, and concludes with a discussion of ACT UP's decline in the early 1990s, foregrounding the role of emotion in these processes throughout.

Your work focuses on AIDS activism but also raises crucial questions about the emotional and affective character of organizing and the limitations of social movement theorizing and left organizing. Can you tell us a bit more about the importance of emotion in movement building and social transformation?

With regard to both social movement theorizing and left organizing, the lure of rationality exerts a lot of force. In terms of theorizing, from the latter half of the 19th century up until the 1970s, social scientists placed emotion at the heart of their accounts of mass movements, but there were a lot of shortcomings with this scholarship. Most problematically, it pitted emotion against reason and depicted protesters as unstable deviants motivated by psychic conflicts and unruly passions.

During the 1970s, scholars who were influenced by the New Left challenged these disparaging pictures of protest and protesters. They created a new field – social movement studies – and developed models of protest as normal political behavior and protesters as rational actors in pursuit of reasonable political goals. These models dominate the field today. Their dispassionate and calculating rational actor has replaced the unthinking and irrational psychological misfit of the earlier literature.

The assumption of rationality certainly was an important corrective, but by assuming rationality and ignoring the emotional dimensions of activism these accounts miss the ways that feelings influence our reasoning selves, contribute to our understandings and thereby shape our sense of what might be politically possible, desirable, and necessary. Rational-actor models miss human motivation that is inchoate, ambiguous, ambivalent, non-coherent and the ways in which human desires, fantasies, attachments, resentments, and anxieties shape political action and inaction. They ignore important phenomena like the euphoria of being in the streets, the intensity of being part of a collectivity, the affective complexities of working with others, and the emotional pedagogies that movements offer their participants. Like others who are trying to bring emotion back into the study of contentious politics, I argue that researchers really cannot understand political action and inaction if they fail to attend to feelings.

With regard to organizing, those of us on the left tend to have enormous faith in rationality. Here's a good example from the US context: when the Downing Street memo was uncovered in 2005, many of us who were against the US war in Iraq thought that this document would turn the public against the war. The memo revealed that George W. Bush wanted to invade Iraq and remove Saddam Hussein as early as July 2002 and that although any justification for military action was weak, his administration was fixing intelligence information in order to make the case. We leftists tend to believe that if given the facts, people will agree with our analysis and possibly even join us. The Downing Street memo did not have that effect, and the reasons why are complex, but one lesson is that "truth" is not the only factor that motivates people's support for leaders, institutions or ideologies. It's not that people are irrational, as those earlier theorists argued, but rather that our political attachments and detachments derive from complex affective states rather than from reason alone. We leftists need to think more about how people's fears, resentments, anxieties, fantasies, desires and aspirations influence our political behavior. The important work that queer theorists have done on the pull of normativity is really useful for thinking about affect and politics.

From my own experience in activist groups, it seems that in addition to this faith in reason, a number of emotional prescriptions and proscriptions operate in many leftist formations. You have to be angry, for example, and there isn't a lot of space for despair. In the case of ACT UP, our work required a hopeful faith in our ability to save lives. That's not a bad thing in itself, but with despair largely *verboten*, we were simply unable to deal with the sense of despair that eventually did take hold. As a result, many participants' experiences remained unacknowledged and unaddressed in the collective space of the movement, and that contributed to the movement's decline.

What were the social and historical circumstances in which the ACT UP groups emerged?

I date the movement's emergence to late 1986. The devastation in lesbian and gay communities was immense by that point, with almost 20,000 dead. Gay men in particular were suffering extreme losses; some had lost their entire social circles to AIDS. The ways in which homophobia was driving the crisis were by then obvious. President Reagan, intent on preserving close relations with leaders of the religious right, had yet to make even one policy speech on AIDS. Funding for research and treatment was utterly inadequate and there were not yet any drugs to treat AIDS. All levels of government were either aggressively ignoring the epidemic or using it as an opportunity to attack those suffering most. Government bodies were increasingly considering punitive laws that called for mandatory HIV-testing and even quarantine. Right-wing pundits like William F. Buckley, Jr. were calling for extreme measures, including tattooing HIV-positive people.

What's a bit puzzling is that these horrors had been present for a while. Queers had been mobilizing in numerous ways but they hadn't yet taken to the streets. A decisive and dramatic shift occurred when the US Supreme Court upheld the constitutionality of the state of Georgia's statute prohibiting homosexual sodomy. Queers were furious. I argue that in the context of ever-increasing AIDS-related deaths, continuing government failure to address the crisis, and increasingly repressive legislation, the *Bowers v. Hardwick* decision in June 1986 transformed lesbian and gay sentiments about themselves, about dominant society, and about what needed to be done to fight the AIDS crisis. And those emotional shifts were crucial in sparking confrontational and defiant direct action AIDS activism.

An important side note is that ACT UP/NY was not the first activist organization to turn to the streets in the fight against AIDS. A group named Citizens for Medical Justice in San Francisco started doing sit-ins and getting arrested in September 1986, six months before ACT UP/NY formed. Two groups in New York, the Lavender Hill Mob and the Silence=Death Project, began acting up in the summer and fall of 1986 respectively, and members from both attended the founding meeting of ACT UP/NY. ACT UP/NY was without a doubt a crucial player in this history, but the movement as a whole did not start with it, as commentators often presume. Neither should the movement be reduced to ACT UP/NY. At the movement's height, there were more than 80 direct-action AIDS activist groups across the US and a few dozen more around the world, including, of course, AIDS ACTION NOW! in Toronto.

How was ACT UP able to link grief, despair, rage, and anger together to develop an empowering direct-action-oriented politics that was sustained until the early 1990s?

Social movements engage in a great deal of what sociologist Arlie Hochschild calls emotion work, which she defines as an attempt to alter one's emotions, to evoke or heighten or suppress a feeling. I use the term to refer to efforts to elicit and alter others' emotions and feelings as well.

ACT UP faced a complex emotional landscape in lesbian and gay communities that included fear of AIDS, immense grief about the accumulating losses, a sense of despair about the relentlessness of the crisis, along with all of the contradictory feelings associated with lesbian and gay ambivalence. After *Bowers* v. *Hardwick* the landscape shifted and gay fury toward the state dramatically intensified. Many queer folks were ready to be done with grief or were at least ripe for channelling their grief into angry activism. ACT UP marshalled this grief and tethered it to anger, and both sentiments to confrontational AIDS activism. It relocated the feeling of pride from its lodging within a politics of respectability to a celebration of sexual difference and confrontational activism. It took on gay shame and suggested that the government should be ashamed of its negligent and murderous response to the AIDS crisis. ACT UP, in other words, offered an emotional pedagogy, ways to feel and to emote. That pedagogy emphasized self-love and self-respect over shame and self-doubt, eased fear of social rejection, challenged the desire for acceptance on straight society's terms and authorized antagonism toward society.

That new matrix of feelings blossomed within ACT UP and provided a "resolution" of sorts to lesbian and gay ambivalence. Although I do not believe that a change in someone's feelings results from simple exhortation – "feel angry!" – I do believe that ACT UP's rhetorical and ritual practices, which expressed, enacted and repeated over and over again this new constellation of feelings, actually affected how people felt. Emotional expression, in other words, has a performative quality. In this case, it not only legitimized those feelings, it also generated them, bringing them into being by naming and enacting them and thereby elevating those emotions while suppressing the negative feeling states that had prevailed earlier.

ACT UP also gave birth to a newly politicized queer sensibility that crystallized this new set of feelings. Foregrounding angry, confrontational activism as well as sex-radicalism and pride in gay difference, queer offered a compelling vision of "how to be gay" in this moment of crisis. All of this emotion work altered what many queer folks were feeling and thereby helped the direct-action AIDS movement to flourish into the 1990s.

How were queers in ACT UP able to hold onto a vibrant sex radicalism in the face of AIDS and pressures within lesbian and gay communities towards sexual respectability?

AIDS intensified the stigma of homosexuality, and many within lesbian and gay communities were understandably anxious about the widespread perception that gay male sexuality itself caused AIDS. Gay newspapers from the 1980s record lesbian and gay politicos issuing multiple challenges to the gay male sexual culture that flowered during the 1970s. The trend was toward sexual respectability, as you say, so ACT UP's sex radicalism was indeed remarkable.

ACT UP wasn't alone, of course. We benefited from the work done by activists who fought against the closure of the bathhouses in 1984 to 1985, from those who invented safer sex (such as the Sisters of Perpetual Indulgence), and from the earlier work of gay liberationists who foregrounded the fight for sexual liberation within a larger social-justice politic.

ACT UP's sex radicalism was a necessary, life-affirming challenge to the equation of queer sex with death. Being in-your-face queer leveled a retort to those who tried to shame and blame gays for AIDS. In a climate where the right was waging war against all things queer, the strategy of denying gay difference not only seemed unviable, it would also simply accede to the right's homophobic logic. Sex-radicalism, then, seemed a vital means to both preserve queer culture and take on the right. Also, the erotic nature of ACT UP is what drew many of us to the group and kept us coming back! It was the place to go to find sexy dykes and fags.

What was the relation of the emergence of ACT UP out of queer communities and notions of camp, humour, and performance in ACT UP activism?

There was a lot of campy humour in ACT UP, and that was surely due to the fact that the movement emerged out of queer communities. How else could we have gone on, given all of the illness and death around us? When I interviewed Marion Banzhaf from ACT UP/NY, she recalled an affinity group satirizing the ACT UP chant "How Many More Must Die?!" when it made a T-shirt that read "Harmony Moore Must Die." The initial chant pointed toward genocide and loss; the satire was silly, an inside joke that helped alleviate the pain of all of that loss. We were living in a climate of bigotry, anti-gay violence, illness, death and unending grief. Campy humour offered all of us much-needed psychic relief and release.

I have a wonderful memory of Ortez Alderson, a member of ACT UP/Chicago, camping it up in a Chicago jail during an action for national health care held in April 1990. Close to 150 AIDS activists from across the country were arrested, effectively overwhelming the city's jail system. Because there were not enough cells for all of us, the police put us into a large room all together. We were euphoric from the protest, happy to be together and there was a lot of animated discussion along with hugging and kissing. Our jubilant conversations quickly reached a high pitch and the officer in charge tried to gain control over the room by demanding that we cease kissing and sit "girl-boy-girl-boy." We giggled at his request and rearranged ourselves like obedient children. Every so often, Ortez would stand up and remind us all, "There is to be noooooo same-sex kissing in the jail," and on cue, we all resumed kissing, boys with boys, girls with girls, girls with boys, gender queers with all. In addition to helping us deal with the deaths occurring all around us, the queer tradition of campy humour bolstered us as we traversed through hostile, anti-gay, anti-radical territory.

How were ACT UP groups able to address questions of gender, race, and class?

People often assume that ACT UP was a white, middle-class, gay male movement, but that ignores that many women, people of colour, working-class people and intersections therein who participated in the movement, and who were in positions of leadership. ACT UP was more diverse than many think.

There were conflicts in the group that revolved around issues of race and racism, and there definitely was racism in the organization, as in any white-dominated group. ACT UP also had its struggles with sexism. Caucuses of women and people of colour formed early on, and sometimes in response to experiences with racism and sexism within ACT UP, but I think there was a sense among many of the women and people of colour, at least during the early years, that ACT UP was a welcoming and receptive environment. Not in the sense that ACT UP was a place free of racism and sexism, but in the sense that it was a place where confronting such issues was seriously engaged. There were many white, anti-racist participants who determinedly and patiently drew attention to the ways that racism was affecting the AIDS epidemic and struggled to get the movement to deal with its own racism. Their perspective had a good deal of legitimacy within ACT UP and succeeded in creating a context in which many white members educated themselves about racism and looked critically at their own racial privilege. The anti-racist, anti-imperialist politics of my closest friends and comrades made ACT UP a crucial site for my own political awakening.

That being said, some of ACT UP's most intense internal conflicts definitely were in part due to racism and sexism. For example, in the early 1990s, an often-repeated claim by some in the movement was that we had gotten "off track," that we were no longer fighting AIDS but instead were fighting racism, sexism, and multiple other social ills, and in doing so were neglecting white gay men with AIDS. Now, it's true that some of us in the movement focused much of our activism on women and people of colour with AIDS. But of course that work was all about AIDS. As a movement committed to fighting AIDS in all of its dimensions, those efforts were not taking the movement off track. But some participants understood those efforts to be "not about AIDS" because such efforts weren't about them. They, understandably, had come to their knowledge of what AIDS was from their particular interests and worries. I don't blame them. In fact, I think complicated feelings of betrayal undergirded their accusations, but their accusations that ACT UP had gotten off track did indicate the presence of a sort of blind racism and sexism within the movement.

Even so, the movement did address many specific concerns of women, people of colour, and poor people with AIDS. That's clear in a years-long campaign that forced the Center for Disease Control to alter the definition of AIDS to include the illnesses that were killing women and poor people with HIV, in the efforts to force the National Institutes of Health to admit women and people of color into experimental drug trials, in the fights to reduce the price of drugs and in all the work around AIDS in prisons. As a movement, we could have done more, but ACT UP did a fairly good job in this realm, largely at the initiative of many women and people of colour in the movement.

What led to the weakening and decline of direct-action AIDS activism and what were its emotional dimensions?

Movements are inseparable from the contexts in which they operate, so in a general sense, changes in a movement's context, and the emotional states generated as a result, can challenge the practices, feelings, imaginaries that organize and constitute that movement, making it difficult for the movement to continue. The emotional states I'm talking about are often fairly amorphous, largely operate beneath conscious awareness, and thus may be difficult to address even as they exert pressure on the movement's existing procedures and rituals that hitherto have worked.

In the early 1990s, ACT UP faced a significantly changed context. First, there was a widespread sense in LGBT communities that greater acceptance from society was forthcoming. That sense produced what I would call an anxious calculus of moderation among gay leaders and other establishment-oriented individuals. ACT UP was never universally loved in LGBT communities, but this sense of political, cultural, and social openings toward gay folks gave discourses against confrontational activism a renewed emotional and psychic force. ACT UP's angry queerness and political and sexual radicalism interfered with the politics of respectability that were being adopted. The community support that ACT UP had enjoyed dissipated as the notion that ACT UP threatened social acceptance gained traction.

A second, probably more important change was ACT UP participants' increasing knowledge of the growing enormity of the AIDS crisis. Douglas Crimp talks about this in terms of our growing knowledge of the many different affected populations and what it was going to take to save all of these people's lives. One consequence of this knowledge was a growing desperation and despair, even as we experienced numerous important victories that were indisputably prolonging people's lives. A scarcity mentality arose within the movement and any focus on one issue or on one population began to be seen as coming at the expense of other people with AIDS. Earlier, ACT UP members had believed that as a movement we could and should take on any and all targets and issues related to the AIDS crisis. But in the changed landscape, others' actions, even when victorious, prompted anxious questions: what about me and the people I care about? This scarcity mentality introduced complex emotional undercurrents into political disagreements about ACT UP's focus that had existed since the start of the movement but that now became personalized and acrimonious. The emotional undercurrents of these conflicts had a tremendous negative impact.

So these two important changes in ACT UP's context created an affective landscape that was hard to navigate. The movement's emotional practices had been oriented primarily toward creating and heightening anger, but different emotion work was called for in this changed context.

Can you say more about those emotional undercurrents? How did moralism and shaming become a destructive force in AIDS activism? Could these tensions have been navigated in a better fashion that we can learn from for our organizing today?

Moralism well-describes the dominant emotional register in which ACT UP's later internal conflicts played out. It unquestionably intensified those conflicts, further unravelled feelings of solidarity and contributed to the demise of the movement. There were shaming accusations that privileged white gay men were only concerned about saving their own lives and those of their friends and thus were liable to sell out other people with AIDS. There were accusations that women and people of colour were in the fight for politics alone and were willing to build a mass movement on the backs, indeed the graves, of gay white men with AIDS. People started invoking identity categories in a way that hadn't happened earlier in the movement's life, essentializing and tethering them to expected identifications and politics. All of that created immense distrust across lines of race, gender, and HIV status.

There has been a lot of critical discussion about political moralism on the left and I find it quite useful. I'm thinking mostly of work by Wendy Brown and Douglas Crimp, but critics frequently fail to illuminate some of the emotional states that prompt a turn toward moralism. To understand the emergence of moralism within ACT UP requires understanding the emotional undercurrents of the movement's internal conflicts. With the term emotional undercurrent I mean to emphasize how the feeling states operating in ACT UP's conflicts were largely unarticulated and submerged, but nevertheless had a force and direction to them that affected the texture, tone, intensity, and velocity of the conflicts. Largely unstated and unacknowledged feelings of betrayal and nonrecognition, and consequent resentment, mistrust and anger were at the heart of the movement's internal conflicts. The presence of those feelings, and the difficulty of dealing with them in part because they were largely unacknowledged, created fertile terrain for shaming and guilt-tripping.

That's not to say that the political conflicts had no substance to them. Members of the different sides had divergent analyses of the AIDS crisis and how best to fight it. But political conflicts in movements are seldom only about divergent political analyses. More than tactical or strategic disagreements, conflicts often revolve around the complex feelings evoked by participants' different statuses within the movement and within society. Whether real or perceived, such differences can generate resentment, anger, guilt, a sense of being unrecognized and fear of betrayal. Left unaddressed, those feelings can prompt a turn to moralizing, which shuts down political debate and principled engagement with one another. In the case of ACT UP, the shaming from both sides displaced conversations about how best to fight AIDS and about what people in the movement were feeling about each other and the crisis. The affects that had sparked the moralizing in the first place, and that were at the core of ACT UP's political conflicts, remained unacknowledged and unaddressed. The moralizing made us unable to approach one another and thus unable to address the conflicts. Both sides demonized the other, personalizing and polarizing what otherwise might have been difficult, but navigable, political conflicts.

Why did we turn to moralism? Well, in part because it was a readily available rhetorical register; Brown calls it the "dominant political sensibility" in this historical period. More specific to ACT UP was the growing despair in the movement. Many of us thought that we were going to be able to save the lives of people with AIDS, but the ever-increasing number of deaths, especially within the movement, pointed to our inability to stop the dying. Moralizing finds fertile ground in a moment of impasse, when activists are politically depressed and grasping for explanations about why their efforts seem futile. Blaming easily morphs into shaming.

Many progressive movements have heated internal conflicts, but conflicts don't inevitably fracture a movement. ACT UP's conflicts became acrimonious in large part because we were unable to address the underlying feelings of betrayal that shaped their substance, velocity, and intensity. On the one hand I would say of course we were unable to address those emotional undercurrents: we all were exhausted, frustrated, desperate, and overwhelmed. But the historian in me knows that the fracturing of solidarity in ACT UP was never inevitable. It may be that assuming solidarity in the early years prevented us from doing more trust-building work in those years. So that's one thing for activist groups to think about. Also, ACT UP's emotional habitus provided us with a pedagogy for some feelings, especially for transforming anger into action, but it did not provide much instruction for dealing with feelings of betrayal by one's comrades, or for dealing with fear of death or an overwhelming sense of despair. Anger was one of our primary idioms, and we turned it against ourselves in a manner that made it difficult to work with one another. This is not about blaming the movement culture, we built but to remind us that the unfolding of the conflicts was contingent. That is true of conflicts in all movements. Studying the dynamics of ACT UP's internal conflicts might allow current activists to address bad feelings that sometimes arise amid the action.

What is the continuing relevance of AIDS activism today?

I haven't been involved in AIDS activism since 1995, but what has really impressed me about groups that have continued the fight is their political savvy in tying local battles to global processes, to global flows of capital. There is really important activism being done that challenges the astronomical pricing of AIDS drugs by transnational pharmaceutical companies and targets trade agreements that put patents and intellectual property rights above the health and well-being of people around the world. These activists are effectively pointing to the link between the worldwide AIDS pandemic and a globalizing capitalist logic that puts profit-seeking above human well-being. They're doing great work.

How do you see the legacy of ACT UP in the context where the mainstream gay and lesbian movements tend to have defined same-sex marriage as the end-point of our struggles?

Oh, gay marriage. One of the most liberating things for me when I started identifying as a lesbian was the realization that now I wouldn't have to get married! ACT UP gave me a similar feeling of freedom and sense of possibility; I think that was true for many who participated in the movement. The politics of anti-normativity that developed within the movement and crystallized in the notion of queer allowed for ways of being in the world that I fear now are disappearing as gay marriage takes over the LGBT movement's agenda. To me, queer, in its most radical sense, was about changing ourselves and the world. It was exhilarating to be involved in that sort of transformative self- and world-making project. That was what ACT UP provided for many of us, and that's an important part of its legacy: we all take those practices and our memories of them out into the world with us, into other activist formations, into our workplaces, into our intimate relations and our everyday interactions. Unfortunately, that queer potential which, in addition to our individualities, is precisely what LGBT folks have to offer to this world, no longer takes pride of place in the gay movement. Queerness has become the bad cousin who has to be renounced and disowned. It's definitely important for us to extend the queer legacy of ACT UP by injecting a queer politic into all of our endeavours.

For those of us who sometimes feel despair regarding the prospects of social change, we should keep in mind that the activism of the direct-action AIDS movement forced enormous changes that have saved people's lives. Saving lives and providing an example of activist victories are tremendous legacies, and recollecting that important history of direct-action AIDS activism can help activists today extend our political horizons. ★

References

Wendy Brown. 2001. *Politics Out of History*. Princeton, NJ: Princeton University Press.

Douglas Crimp. 1992. "Right On, Girlfriend!" *Social Text* 33:2–18.

Douglas Crimp. 2002. *Melancholia and Moralism: Essays on AIDS and Queer Politics*. Cambridge, MA: MIT Press.

Arlie Russell Hochschild. 1979. "Emotion Work, Feeling Rules, and Social Structure." *American Journal of Sociology* 85, no. 3:551–75.

Movements Where
People Can Grow

An Interview with Helen Hudson

Helen Hudson is a queer Black anti-authoritarian organizer living in Montreal. For over a decade she has been actively involved in immigration, prisoner justice, queer, trans and feminist struggles, and student organizing. She spent four years working as the coordinator of QPIRG Concordia, an activist resource centre at Concordia University that serves as a central hub for student and community activists in Montreal. Currently, Hudson participates on the board of the Institute for Anarchist Studies, the Montreal Anarchist Bookfair collective, and the Certain Days Political Prisoner Calendar collective. She also works full-time as a nurse.

This interview is based on a conversation between Helen Hudson and Chris Dixon. A longtime anti-authoritarian activist and writer, Dixon spent more than ten years on the US West Coast where he was active in student, global justice, anti-racist, labour, and anti-war organizing efforts. Dixon initiated this conversation as part of a project in which he traveled across Canada and the US to talk with other anti-authoritarian organizers about their work, challenges, and insights. Although what follows includes mainly Hudson's contributions, these developed out of a joint exploration of their organizing experiences.

How would you describe your politics?

Although I don't shy away from formal or intellectual descriptions, I still have a very hard time pinning down what I believe. I know what it is when I organize with people and see who I have affinity with and who I don't. When I define how I organize on that basis,

I find myself organizing with people who call themselves feminists and with people for whom all forms of oppression are central to their politics. Since coming to Montreal nine years ago, where the parameters are quite different than in English Canada, I keep ending up in organizations with "anarchist" in the title. I value organizing in anti-authoritarian ways that try to include people in decisions to the degree that they're affected by the outcome. I value autonomy and self-determination but also community, solidarity.

I don't have a very detailed vision of the exact kind of society I'd like to see, but I think the things that I value in organizing are the things I would value in a society. My hope is that if we address injustices now and organize in a just way, the society that follows will be the kind of society that I would want. I think that's going to take an incredibly long time. I don't necessarily see that achieved in my lifetime.

Some of the older organizers whose vision I really respect describe how certain they were in the sixties and seventies that the revolution was happening, and that they were going to see the type of society they wanted if they just gave it their all. They took incredible risks and did incredible things because they really thought it was very, very close. And I can see in world events at that time that it would make sense to think it was that close. Looking back, I see where they were coming from. On the other hand, I can't fathom how anyone could have possibly thought that capitalism was about to fall. Capitalism was, and still is, quite robust and very good at adapting.

I want to learn from people's mistakes, people's disappointments, and people's misjudgments. I do want to be ready to give it my all, to give up things that I value, to take risks when it's clear that it's the moment to do so. But I also think it's really important to organize sustainably and view this as something I'm going to be doing for the rest of my life. Similarly, I have to transmit what I'm doing to people who are younger than me because they're going to be doing it for the rest of their lives. I'm not necessarily going to see the end result of it beyond the fact that doing it is its own end result. I'd much rather be living as an organizer, in the communities I'm involved with, than doing something else.

What does effective organizing look like to you?

Key to effective organizing is doing something that's concrete and tangible to organizers with a long-term vision, to people who are newly politicized, and to whoever's affected – whether it's in a neighborhood or a campus or a prison or a workplace. To be effective, the goals have got to be clear to all those different participants, wherever they're at in their level of consciousness of the political process.

I'm never sure how much of a distinction is useful between organizers as such, and people who are part of the community where the organizing is occurring. I do feel like consciousness is part of politics. I've heard the argument that everybody who is oppressed is conscious of their oppression and will therefore rise up and take back the world. I think that's true to a degree. But being explicitly aware of the dynamics of oppression and exploitation, and then consciously acting to address them is a key part of being an organizer, or at least a participant in a movement, versus someone who's part of an oppressed or exploited class, community, group, etc. So based on that belief, I think that effective organizing needs to recognize and speak to those differing levels of consciousness.

This idea was first apparent to me as I became involved in the student movement. In the mid 90s, tuition rose sharply in Canada, so in addition to those who were ideologically opposed to tuition, we began to see more and more people for whom it was a matter of "can I afford to come back to school next year?" In that instance it was relatively easy to build a campaign where the goal – a tuition freeze – encompassed both the tangible and the abstract in a way that was politically consistent. Although we weren't successful in freezing (let alone abolishing) tuition, the fact that we were consistent in our politics did manage to politicize people in a way that lasted beyond the specific campaign.

More recently, I think of some of the challenges we've faced in migrant justice organizing, working with individuals or families who have very concrete concerns: they may have an imminent deportation date, they may be in detention, or maybe they don't have access to vital medical care. We need to attend to those concerns, but also realize that doing so could keep us busy from now to eternity without ever addressing the larger oppressive system that draws us (as solidarity organizers, people who have papers) to these struggles – actually working towards status for all or for open borders.

Sometimes there's been an effective balance of both factors. The campaign by non-status Algerians and their allies between 2002 and 2004 managed to win papers for the vast majority of those that sought them. It changed the terrain of non-status organizing in Montreal and launched a new level of mobilization around migrant justice. I was only peripherally involved in that campaign, but it strikes me that this balance existed in part because of external factors. When Canada lifted its moratorium on deportations to Algeria, about a thousand people suddenly faced deportation within a very short time. So the tangible-goal side of the equation was pretty much covered. Those thousand people were not that hard to mobilize. But the role of the solidarity organizers was also key. Some non-Algerians were very involved in the campaign, and they debated with their Algerian comrades about the politics, the strategy, and the tactics of the campaign. As a result of these debates, as well as the lived experience of struggle, some of the Algerians remained mobilized well after they got their papers. I don't think those same material conditions have reoccurred since the non-status Algerians' campaign, and as a result, that balance between concrete concerns and broader political goals is a tension that continues to be debated, rather than something that's been adequately resolved.

What kinds of organizations and institutions do you think we should be building? Are there particular features or forms of organization that you think are important?

Organizing, movement-building to end capitalism is much more effective if there is an explicit, concrete form of organization. I'm talking about a radically democratic organization that exists over time, explicitly has a membership, explicitly has a set of politics, and has, for want of a better term, a process of membership development, so that people are doing the concrete tasks of organizing together while also learning how to do these tasks. There are lots of tangible skills that you learn informally over time. But we need a systematic way of making sure that people learn, for example, how to make a speech, how to do a door-to-door campaign, how to design a poster, how to write effectively, how to mobilize a bunch of people to fight around a demand, how to facilitate a meeting. It's a huge limitation that we don't have a formalized way of doing that.

I'd also like to see us be a lot clearer about how we can relate to organizations over which we have no direct ownership. The sorts of organizations I just finished talking about would be autonomous of any kind of state structure or structure outside of the movement. But how do we relate to organizations that can be a resource but aren't autonomous? For example, the PIRG (Public Interest

Research Group) at Concordia University does a lot of things for organizers. I think that's great, but its funding comes from a source external to the movement – the student body of Concordia. When backlash occurs, that funding can be gone. When I was on staff at the Concordia PIRG, the political terrain on campus was quite left. Even in the backlash that followed 9/11, the PIRG was able to continue to function fairly well as a resource for organizers both on and off campus despite certain constraints. But I've seen a couple of PIRGs lose their funding, and many more have had to put significant energy into fighting against de-funding campaigns. So I've come to realize that we can't operate as if we own those organizations. I do think we should continue to use them but we also need to be aware of the gap between the politics of the funders and those setting the group's direction. The same is true of any organization with government or union funding. I think having a much higher consciousness and an explicit shared understanding about how we relate to those useful organizations that aren't owned by the movement would be really helpful.

A third thing that we need is a series of institutions where we can, as a movement, explicitly and concretely elaborate theory, tools, and organizing approaches that can then be systematically shared among people and movements. This is what draws me to the Institute for Anarchist Studies (IAS), an organization whose purpose is to foster the elaboration of theory. The various methods the IAS uses to work toward this goal – its journal, the writing grants it provides to radical thinkers, and the annual Renewing the Anarchist Tradition conference it hosts – often seem less immediately important than working on frontline campaigns. But without theory, those frontline campaigns tend to flounder. We reinvent the wheel, or repeat the same mistakes over and over again.

Could you talk about the dichotomy that frequently gets set up between "reform work" and "radical work." How do we prioritize struggles to improve the lives of directly affected people while also retaining our radical vision?

I think we always need to be up front about why we're doing what we're doing. When we were fighting the tuition increases in Ontario in the 90s, the vast majority of people that came out to the rallies were opposed to the increases. But organizers were explicit that we were fighting the tuition hike because of the principle of accessibility to education. Not only did we not want tuition to go up, we didn't want tuition to exist. Our demand to the university, as we occupied the president's office, as we disrupted the board of governors meeting, was not "zero tuition now"; it was a freeze on the current tuition level. That was something we could rally more people around, but we were very clear that we wanted zero tuition. We were also very clear that, even with zero tuition, we would not have an accessible education because of all those things that make the University of Guelph, as it existed then and does now, inaccessible. We were talking about race and class and gender, about pedagogy and how the university is set up, and about the division of labor in the university. But we were talking about all of these issues in the speeches at the rallies against that specific tuition hike. We didn't call a rally for an open university with radical pedagogy because nobody was going to come to that sort of rally in 1997 in Guelph.

We have to prioritize talking about why we're doing what we're doing and engaging people who are new to organizing. Things become reformist when the vast majority only see the specific goal and don't connect it to something larger. There's another element to this: all of these political goals are underpinned by caring about people – believing that everybody is good or can be good. I believe in the potential of everybody to be radicalized. There's a lot in the world that makes people build up walls, especially in contexts in which people are oppressors at the same time as being oppressed, which is most of the time. But I think that struggle can be a really humanizing experience. If you're struggling around a single-issue reform, but you organize yourself in such a way that the process is transformative for the people involved, then I think that's what can make it non-reformist.

You're saying that, through struggle, we experience our own humanity and the humanity of others in a really profound way.

Yeah, and in a really engaged way. I think a democratic society would look a lot like the way our movement is set up: people argue about things or elaborate what position would be the right position and try to convince each other. To be really engaged with your community is to have the kind of debates that are necessary to the movement, but I think they're also necessary to any community. If there's a problem or an injustice, you talk about it until it's worked out. And that's not always pretty. Sometimes horrific things happen in communities and people get really hurt. But I think engaging with that is a more human and humanizing experience than the ways in which mainstream society deals with injustice most of the time.

I've seen some feminist organizations I've been involved with really grapple with racism and transphobia in ways that were definitely hard, and sometimes caused deep rifts. But enough people stuck with the issue that real change was able to happen. All of the groups I've been part of that operated as women's centres have since rethought their mandates to address the ways that patriarchy oppresses through transphobia as well as sexism. And at the same time, an analysis of white supremacy has become more commonplace in gender centres. These struggles are ongoing, but that's sort of my point: there's a willingness, at least on the part of some, to see this ever-developing politic as part of how these spaces operate.

It sounds like prefigurative politics, the idea that we should build ways of relating and social structures that reflect the kind of society that we want to create. How do you deal with the inherent contradiction that we can never build the perfect society in our movement as long as we have to keep fighting at the same time?

At the same time as we're living in this movement, we're living in this unjust world and we continue to soak up the poison of that, however much we fight against our own tendencies to be oppressive. It's going to continue to seep in and we're going to continue to be oppressed, both by the oppressive tendencies of other people in the movement and by the rest of the world we live in.

I see modeling what we want the world to be in our movement as key. Of all the ways we need to do that, one of the things I think we're the worst at is having a very explicit structure. It's also striking to me that we're not that principled or caring in the way we treat each other. For example, if you look at discourses around security culture, there are very useful types of lists and tools that have been developed for how to treat each other specifically related to movement security. Similarly, quite a few "do's and don'ts" lists and "how to" tools have been developed for responding to sexual assault in activist communities. Sometimes I think there just needs to be one overarching list of all the things we need to do all the time, period. The fact that we don't owes, in part, to the fact that we don't have an explicit, structured commitment to each other in a formal "we are in an organization" kind of way.

I think there's humility and a lot of trust involved in treating people really well. And I think one of the things that oppression does is rob people of that trust. I don't deny people their right to or justification for having a self-protective shell or being angry or putting themselves before others because I see how people have to do that to survive. But I feel like when I do that, I'm not surviving; it just makes me profoundly depressed to not be able to care for and trust people.

Are there particular examples that you feel are useful and replicable for developing healthy anti-oppression politics within groups and movement spaces?

For some reason, concrete examples don't spring to mind as readily as lessons I feel I've drawn from working to undo oppression. Firstly, whatever else happens, it's key that oppression be worked through and dismantled within the context of friendships. If people are going to anti-oppression workshops, reading the right books, and challenging each other on their behaviors, but they don't also have close friends who really love them and trust them and whom they really love and trust, with whom they can talk about the ways that they're being oppressive and really start to practice and model and learn other ways of being, it's going to go nowhere. You can go to all the anti-oppression workshops you want, and read everything by everybody who has written good things about it, but it's not going to go anywhere if you can't stay up late in the night talking with someone about this dynamic where you realize you're being oppressive but you're not really sure how to work through it.

Secondly, I think it's important to talk about oppression as a concept, but also specific forms of oppression – transphobia, sexism, racism, ableism, and others – and the particular ways in which those things play out. There are commonalities but there are also important differences. It's important to talk about those things explicitly because otherwise you miss the importance of each particular history and each specific set of power differentials. That being said, it's also important to keep sight of the underlying goal of treating people well, and treating them justly.

When we're addressing oppression within the movement, I think sometimes the fact that we're operating within a community that we're committed to, that we love, gets lost. I understand why it gets lost. I'm not trying to say, "why can't people be nicer to their oppressors?" Of course people are going to be angry. Of course people aren't going to feel committed to oppressors that don't even realize that anything is going on. However, the models I've seen most often for people of a particular oppressed group within a larger organization trying to address that type of oppression – it's just this fast-burning flame that burns itself out and ends in a severing of the ties between the oppressed group and the other people. I'm most interested in seeing how you can find, but also how you can reach out to and nurture, the few allies that will be able to offer a bridge. An important task for those allies is to do that friendship thing I was talking about. And that only works if a general framework or skeleton of that type of friendship exists in community to begin with. It has to happen before a crisis occurs. It's not going to work to build it once people are in conflict and emotions are flaring.

To come back to an earlier point, part of the problem with not having formal structured movement organization is that when oppressive behaviors explode, it's very easy for people to just move on, saying "okay, I'm not welcome in this community. I'll go organize somewhere else." If the various movement organizations and spaces are all connected, we can't do that.

In your political practice, how do you relate to the question of leadership?

I want to talk about the concept of elders. Most of the time this will mean people who are older but what's key for me in the concept is people who have been organizing longer, people who have seen things in organizing that others maybe haven't seen yet. I think the state actively tries to separate generations of organizers. One of the things that keeps movements down is having to reinvent the wheel and not having a sense of history. We can partly address this by having institutions, but we also need to connect with people from whom there are lessons to be learned. This has been fundamental to my own political development. Those elders include the political prisoners I work with on the *Certain Days* calendar, radical professors I've encountered as a student, or simply more experienced organizers with whom I've crossed paths. However, the anti-authoritarian left in North America remains in many ways a youth culture and so it's not always easy to connect with elders – we have to seek them out. In fact, my analysis of the way that the state uses political imprisonment is that it is designed to disrupt intergenerational connections. Prison isolates the prisoners from support, but also deprives younger generations of radicals from the experience of revolutionaries who have much to teach us.

That being said, a "generation" of organizers can be a fairly narrow age-range. When I speak of generations, I'm not necessarily talking about a 20 year age gap. People who I wouldn't think of as being from a different generation, culturally, can be marked by very different world events in terms of their politics. For example, I think of the first few years that I was in Montreal as being marked by the anti-globalization movement, which gave folks who radicalized before or during that time the context to develop a certain analysis of transnational capital, but also a different context for developing skills in direct action street tactics, a different relationship to police at demonstrations.

So while I don't really think of myself as an elder, at a certain point I noticed that a lot of people I organize with have been organizing for a lot less time than I have. And I think there are concrete skills that need to be shared and need to be passed on. One form of leadership is considering it a central political responsibility to pass on what has been learned. I'm still fairly uncomfortable with that role myself, but I do see that as a form of leadership that folks of my "generation" need to begin to grow into: passing on what we've learned, as well as continuing to seek out what can be learned.

During the upsurge of summit mobilizations, there was a rich conversation about tactics, but almost no conversations about strategy. Do you have any ideas about how we can generate more strategic thinking?

Something I see in Montreal is we have a lot of fairly short-lived projects and collectives. In fact, if you're talking about summit mobilizations, what I noticed in Montreal is that while a lot was learned in mobilizing for the Summit of the Americas in Quebec City, there's been a certain re-inventing of the wheel. Montrealers were very involved in mobilizing for the Take the Capital! convergence in 2002 when the G8 met in Kananaskis; there was the WTO mini-ministerial meeting in Montreal in 2003, and other summits since then for which we definitely applied much of the organizing model used in 2001. A lot of the same people were involved, but what struck me as more of these convergences happened was that there was not any structural continuity per se. There was a template: one or more Consultas, or large planning assemblies, the group would come up with a set of principles which tended to be quite similar from one convergence to the next, and then the mobilizing would proceed from there. With each convergence we refined our skills and our analysis, and there was quite a significant overlap in the people, but there was never one organization that provided continuity in structure or in politics from one to the next.

In fairness, I should mention that there was a definite effort to keep the Convergence des Luttes Anti-Capitalistes (CLAC) functional after the Summit of the Americas, and I should also mention that the methodology of starting the process more or less anew each time was in part a purposeful decision in the name of having an open, democratic process. But it also felt to me as if there was an element of reactiveness to it, and after several rounds of this it began to feel to me like we were losing some of what we built each time we disbanded. That ephemeral quality is not unique to organizing around summits.

I think people are pretty okay with having a strategy on the level of a campaign, where a demo is a tactic or a press conference is a tactic; the specific acts are tactics and we have a larger strategy of how we're approaching this campaign. But on a larger level, if you see the campaign as a tactic – so for example, the tactic of disrupting a meeting of global capital – it's not so clear where we're going. What's the larger strategy behind all these mobilizations?

Part of what makes that difficult is that we don't have that ongoing organization. If the campaign itself is the largest level of organization that exists, your strategy is restricted to getting from the beginning to the end of that campaign. Within that, you have the specific things you do – the tactics. As another example, we might decide that whenever someone from Stephen Harper's cabinet shows up, we're going to disrupt him or, if there's a deportation, we're going try to stop it. In terms of the tactics, we might use demos, press conferences, community assemblies. But if the entirety of what you're trying to do is that campaign and that's the largest thing for which you have a structure, then you can't think bigger than that.

The only larger thing that people with whom I organize in Montreal have, other than those campaigns or sets of demands (like "status for all" or "abolish the security certificates"), are principles that are common from campaign to campaign: we think that autonomy and self-determination are important; we think it's important to include an analysis of all forms of oppression. But those things are so wide. We need structures to bridge those broad principles and those specific on-the-ground actions, and

I have no idea what those would be. That's just something I've never experienced in an anti-authoritarian context. I have to admit, I do think there's a lot to be learned from authoritarian leftist organizations sometimes. If there would be some way to take a good, structured, in-depth look at how some of the least problematic far-left political parties are set up and then take what we like from that, that could be useful.

That we keep reinventing the wheel on the specific campaign level and never get to a larger strategy ties very directly to burnout and lack of sustainability. We don't even have continuity of people beyond five years most of the time. The utility of having organizational continuity doesn't cross most people's minds because they're not around long enough to see the wheel being reinvented. If somebody's involvement starts after the beginning and concludes before the end of a given campaign, then how could they possibly see the need for something larger than that campaign?

As you grow older and look ahead to a life in struggle, how do you think about sustaining yourself for the long haul?

I think there's this great reticence on a lot of people's parts to establish a capital "L" life – something that people seem to equate with "selling out," or ceasing to be part of the movement and start being a "regular person." But I think those two ideas need to brought together if we're going to sustain ourselves individually and as a movement. One of the things that worries me is that a lot of the people I organize with are not actually going be okay – concretely, in terms of food or shelter – because they're not thinking past forty. I'm talking financially, but also about the way they build relationships – family, in the broader sense of the word – because we're such a transient movement. Sometimes I think, well, others in the movement, myself included, will be there to support them. But we're not going to be able to look after everybody. The proportion of people who are setting themselves up in such a way that they could do so is just too small.

When I look around, I see a lot of people who are really not thinking about how they're going to survive materially or emotionally beyond the headlong rush into the next demo. It worries me to think about how people I care about are going to survive in the long-term. It's certainly not encouraged by "peer pressure," for lack of a better term. In fact, it's actively discouraged. To be clear, I don't think everybody needs to go to university and get a job and set up an RSP, etc. Also, not everybody can. There's this whole conversation about privilege to be had there. But I think seeing your own long term survival – materially, emotionally, and relationally – as somehow being in conflict with commitment to the movement is just a bad idea. It's not realistic.

And it's not just people getting old, either. In other instances, people get quite seriously ill. There are some comrades who rally around them – go over and make them dinner and do their dishes and accompany them to the hospital or give them money when they need it – but it's a small subset of organizers. There are a number of people that spring to mind who, currently or recently, have disappeared from the activist scene, and people are like, "oh, whatever happened to so and so?" And it's because so and so is really ill or their parents died, and we're not able to have them still be an integrated part of our community.

For me, the question of sustainability brings up the concept of family. Family is a pretty loaded concept; there's tons there to unpack. Organizers I know have a wide range of relationships to their families of origin and to the concept of family. To take a Marx-and-Engels analysis of the family, I think there's a lot of validity to saying that family is part of the problem. But, with respect to sustainability in long-term struggle, I think that having some kind of intergenerational connection – a unit of support that you know is always going to be there, whether that's organized biologically, romantically, or in some other way – is so key for me. If more organizers could have that, I think it would definitely be good. There's a lot we could do in the movement to create that.

One of the contexts in which I've seen organizers treat each other most oppressively is in their romantic relationships. I think that's one of the things that causes people to drop out as well. Generally speaking, if the people you're trying to build a better world with are just not good to each other, that can make you question why you're organizing at all. But when it happens in the most intimate of settings, then it's just utterly destroying. I see my personal life as existing within the movement. That necessarily means that I want my romantic relationships to be political spaces. But then, when things fall apart, it definitely affects organizing. I've seen too many good organizers – mostly women – leave the movement because of this.

The other way that there is a disconnect between the more positive conceptions of family and the way we're organizing is when people have kids. It seems to be difficult for people to get past the notion of family as a nuclear unit. It's one thing to have childcare for meeting and another to make time to homeschool your kid or deal with your kid's school or health problems. All of this goes beyond taking narrowly defined collective responsibility for childcare. So many parents – mostly moms – disappear when the wider community doesn't create space for children and parents. Fortunately, I'm starting to see some really heartening work around collective child-rearing.

The other concept that your question brings up for me is healing. The things that mark my political development are things that also could have destroyed me – traumatic events but also the dynamics of racism and growing up queer but more or less closeted. I think the degree to which movements can be healing – and the degree to which there's space for that, for it to be messy but still okay – is directly proportional to the sustainability of the movement and the ability for people to stay involved.

Through my involvement in gender centres, I've counseled a lot of people dealing with personal trauma, some of whom were also organizers and others who were not. I've noticed that taking action to address not only your own oppression, your own trauma, but also the way that same oppression is manifested more broadly in society can be really empowering, really healing. Some radical communities seem more willing to make space for that than others. I mention this because the gender centre example is perhaps overly obvious. But even radical spaces that don't explicitly place healing at the centre of their praxis, can – and I think should – foster that type of self-awareness and empowerment.

I noticed for myself, as a person of colour and as someone who spent a chunk of my childhood living under military dictatorship, that my relationship to armed agents of the state in general and riot cops in particular, changed over the period when anti-globalization organizing peaked. By confronting riot cops in the street, and then having spaces to think through those interactions – in affinity group debriefing sessions, in direct action workshops, and in informal discussions – I became able to place myself in situations that I previously would have avoided. If our movements can provide spaces where people can grow, can learn about themselves and become more self-actualized, those movements will be more sustainable both on an individual and collective level. ★

Going For Broke

OCAP and the Economic Crisis

John Clarke

For nearly two decades, the Ontario Coalition Against Poverty (OCAP) has been working to mobilize resistance in some of Toronto's poorest communities. These years have been marked by a concerted drive by capitalist governments at every level to cut social programs and to transfer wealth from the poorest in society to the richest. Using methods of direct collective action, OCAP has fought to defend individuals and families whose rights have been denied. We mobilize to oppose cutbacks to social services, and to demand adequate income levels and affordable housing. We resist the drive to push poor and homeless people out of their neighbourhoods in the interest of upscale urban redevelopment. During this time, we have gained a body of experience and built a base in poor communities. Now, as a deep economic crisis begins to take effect, we are facing the challenge of adapting our work and developing new methods of resistance on a transformed scale. What follows is an attempt to look at how the downturn is likely to impact Toronto's poor and to examine some of the forms of fighting back that can emerge in this new political period.

It was only a few months ago that Prime Minister Harper was dismissing the possibility of a serious economic downturn. He wouldn't care to go to a meeting of G8 leaders today and repeat such a laughable assertion. We are now seeing the impact of capitalism's crisis. Employment insurance offices in Toronto are full of newly unemployed people trying to see if the program can offer them any help. They are, for the most part, finding that they have been cut adrift and that they do not qualify for benefits. Welfare caseloads are registering their first major increases in Toronto, with a 10 percent jump in applications in February 2009. The depths of suffering and the extent of dislocation will increase massively in the months ahead.

It is important to recognize that this crisis is not comparable to the economic recessions of the 1980s and 1990s. Not only is it a more fundamental manifestation of the contradictions of capitalism, but it is taking effect after decades of neoliberalism. The international neoliberal offensive has been devoted to altering the balance of forces in society and removing those limited barriers to profit-making that the postwar compromise created. For this very reason, it destroyed many of the factors that might have lessened the impact of the economic downturn and drastically altered the bases on which resistance to it might have emerged.

There are several major considerations that flow from the legacy of neoliberalism. Systems of social provision, particularly those relating to income support for the unemployed and poor, have been a major target of neoliberal policy-makers. This shredding of the "social safety net" will be a hugely significant factor in framing the nature of the struggle that emerges. We are also dealing with a greatly changed situation created by the weakening of working class organizations. Unions have been hit hard and their leaderships are far more conservative than they were a decade ago. The immediate prospects for rank-and-file challenges to these increasingly weak and collaborationist organizations are not heartening. Economically, the working class is divided into those who have barely maintained living standards by working harder and longer and accessing credit as never before and those who have lost their jobs and are reliant on the inadequacies of social assistance or have been driven into the ranks of the homeless. For most working class people, the call to collective action is more often than not outweighed by individual efforts to survive.

The question that underlies the current situation is: "Now that capitalism is in crisis, who is going to pay for it?" The left's liberal thinkers who see this situation as an impending return to the glory days of Keynesian class compromise are sadly mistaken. It is true that the reckless deregulation of the recent past has been called into question and that some level of "stimulation spending" has become the mainstream view of those in economic and political power. Liberal Party leader Michael Ignatieff and New Democratic Party leader Jack Layton realized this quicker than Prime Minister Stephen Harper and his Finance Minister Jim Flaherty. However, those who watched the federal budget brought before Parliament and deemed acceptable by the Liberals have seen the two main political formations of the ruling class in Canada ready to go into this crisis with the system of unemployment insurance so greatly reduced that it fails to cover the great majority of the unemployed. The Ontario budget is similarly dismissive of the needs of working-class people. To date, no mainstream political party has demonstrated any intention of improving income support programs to prevent an explosion of poverty and destitution.

It is also important to realize that the sudden frenzied resolve to print money and bail out major financial institutions and sections of the manufacturing sector does not signify benevolence on the part of those in power. The state has always stood ready to underwrite the major organizations of capital and to use public resources to stabilize them. Moreover, as recent developments in the auto industry show us, the measures they take will at every turn and to an increasing degree be used to force massive austerity programs on workers, crushing the already weakened capacity of trade unions to defend working class interests. Even where money may be pumped into initiatives related to basic infrastructure, we can't expect the needs of workers and poor communities to be at the forefront. We can be certain that the focus will continue to be on profit driven schemes that reflect corporate priorities and that undermine wages and working conditions for workers.

In the United States, the newly established Obama administration has given rise to false hopes, but the situation is fundamentally the same. Only in terms of its deceptive rhetoric and minor gestures will the actions of the US government reflect the need to protect working class people from the impacts of this crisis. Some of the assumptions of the neoliberal era have been questioned by its architects but tactical shifts notwithstanding, the goal of increasing the rate of exploitation has been preserved. Indeed, an explosion in unemployment rates and a heightened level of vulnerability will be seen as a golden opportunity to press forward even more ruthlessly than before with attacks on unions, wage cuts and the undermining of social programs.

Under the impact of this crisis, shock waves are passing through whole communities of people and their organizations. These shocks will be felt most profoundly by low-income communities in crisis and under attack even before the markets imploded. There have been predictions, based on the history of the Great Depression, that we may expect a significant period of shocked passivity to unfold in response to the situation that is taking shape. But we can't automatically conclude that things will develop along the same lines today. Organizing social resistance and struggle is not like sitting on a platform waiting for a train to come in. If no lead is given, passivity is more likely than resistance. If, on the other hand, there are efforts to develop political education, agitation and models of effective resistance, shock can give way to anger and a readiness to fight back. At this point, we should look closely at how this crisis is playing out in working class communities of Ontario.

As workplace closures and massive layoffs develop, we need to consider the drastic and protracted process of weakening unemployment insurance in Canada. The experiences of the recently unemployed are going to have particular elements to them and they will be a volatile grouping for definite reasons. The fact that most of the unemployed can't collect unemployment insurance – or employment insurance (EI) as it has been humorously renamed – means that the downturn in the economy will generate a population of people who are waiting to be poor enough to collect welfare. When EI offices turn them away, they will discover that welfare pays a sub-poverty pittance and even this will not be available to them. Welfare is a means-tested system and, if you have any level of savings or assets, you must use those up before you can apply. There is something truly explosive about the kind of bitterness, anger, and desperation that will develop among people who watch their homes and savings being taken from them. It will be driven into their minds that there is no support for them and that they have been abandoned by the system.

Once people have exhausted their savings and reached a level of poverty that enables them to apply for the post-Harris welfare payments, they will find them difficult to access. Welfare is a restrictive and arbitrary system that turns away a high proportion of applicants, even when they are ostensibly eligible under the system's own rules. People are not told of benefits that would help them and inquiries about such benefits are met with evasion and deceit. Applicants are denied basic assistance and recipients have their benefits cut off on grounds that have no justification under legislation and regulations that the welfare offices claim to be implementing. There is a fundamental uncertainty about what is required to be eligible for welfare, which operates as an additional barrier to accessing welfare, thereby saving the government money and at the same time forming one of the "rituals of degradation" that give the system its punitive character.

It is to be expected that every effort will be made to restrict access to welfare. In Toronto, under the self-styled "progressive" administration of David Miller, the contingency fund for the city's welfare system has been reduced from $90 million to a mere $8 million. As welfare caseloads explode, the ability of the city to meet its obligation to pay 20 percent of the cost of the program will be called into question. An indication of the impending attack on those in need of welfare has recently emerged. OCAP has worked very hard to help people access a food allowance within the welfare system that goes under the name of the Special Diet. This monthly social assistance benefit was set up to help people – who are able to obtain an appropriate medical diagnosis – meet their basic food needs. Since 2005, we have organized community health clinics through which thousands of people have obtained the Special Diet funds. We have also organized hundreds of direct actions to successfully resist attempts by welfare offices to deny these benefits. When we took up this fight, $2 million a year in Special Diet income was going to people on welfare in Toronto. This year benefits have increased to $4.1 million a month. In March 2009, following a *Toronto Sun* column that alleged "scammers" were obtaining the Special Diet improperly, the city's auditor was called in to look for ways to limit access to this vital program. If taking food away from the poorest families in Toronto is the kind of "cost-saving measure" the city will adopt to weather the downturn then we are in for a very harsh period indeed.

Recent media reports show a significant increase in food bank use. For years, food banks and other charitable operations have functioned as a de facto back-up system that masks the gross inadequacy of welfare payments. Without food banks, the full impact of government cutbacks would result in dramatically increased rates of housing evictions and levels of malnutrition. With mounting caseloads and growing numbers of people being denied welfare assistance, the demand for food bank services will continue to grow, but there is no reason to expect that these charities will be able to extend their services beyond their current limited capacity.

The largest landlord in Toronto is the municipally run Toronto Community Housing (TCH), with 180,000 people living in its units. The fact that such a large number of poor people have access to rent-geared-to-income accommodation is a considerable factor in terms of who can get and maintain housing in Toronto. This housing option, however, is in the process of being deliberately eliminated. TCH housing is in a massive state of disrepair and TCH acknowledges that it would need to spend $300 million to bring its housing up to the basic standards that provincial legislation demand of landlords. Since neither the city or provincial governments have provided adequate funding, TCH housing is being allowed to reach a level of dilapidation that will justify a Regent Park-style "revitalization" by private developers. The housing will be pulled down and replaced with developer-built condominiums possessing a "rent-geared-to-income component" that can be reduced and eventually eliminated. Now TCH is increasing the pace of this form of redevelopment and is also moving to sell off the individual homes that it owns throughout the city. With the loss of revenue that so many people face, this threat to the future of public housing is bound to be devastating.

Before the present crisis hit the markets, there were already about 20 percent more evictions from rental accommodations in Ontario under Premier Dalton McGuinty than under former Premier Mike Harris. It needs to be understood what a serious indicator this is in the present situation. People will do just about anything to retain their housing. They will certainly cut expenditures on all other items, including food, before they get put on the streets. For every person who is evicted, there are many others who are within sight of the same fate and staving it off with great difficulty. Job losses, wage cuts, and the denial of social benefits all feed the housing problem. As these factors come more into play, it is to be expected that the scale of evictions will increase and that the problem will assume the proportions of a crisis. At the same time, a dramatic increase in evictions will constitute a major flashpoint for community-based resistance.

A serious increase in homelessness points to another area where the attacks of the recent past have cast their shadow over the developing crisis. Toronto has been generating an oversupply of upscale housing for the past 20 years. As a result, the drive to clear low-income populations from their neighbourhoods and disperse homeless people in order to make way for affluent newcomers has become a defining feature of urban life. The restriction of homeless shelters, particularly in the downtown core, has been a high priority for the political servants of redevelopment. Shelters are already hopelessly inadequate to deal with the size and needs of the homeless population. The downturn will put more people on the streets, including those who come to Toronto from smaller centres that lack the infrastructure to deal with the problem of destitution. In the months ahead we have to organize to ensure that there are available places of shelter for everyone that needs housing.

No One is Illegal – Toronto (NOII-Toronto), the main organization in Toronto that defends the rights of those who live here without legal status, recently organized a series of events under the slogan of "the city is a sweatshop." The goal of this project was to continue the group's challenge of racism and racist immigration laws that are used to obtain maximum profits from the most vulnerable workers and to point out that the basic provisions of Ontario's Employment Standards Act are ignored with near impunity. One of the central features of an economic downturn, of course, is that it massively reduces the bargaining power of workers. That is true even of those who are organized in unions. For those who are unorganized and precariously employed and, even more, for those who are without status and living in Canada under the threat of arrest and deportation, the downturn will place formidable power in the hands of their employers. Sub-minimum wage employment is likely to proliferate and vulnerable workers will face greater abuses as the crisis develops.

The crisis will also entail increased police repression. While just about every system of social provision has been progressively dismantled over the last number of years, Toronto's police budget has swollen to the point where it is the largest area of city spending. It will soon be an obscene $1 billion per year item. David Miller has bragged to the media that there are more cops on the streets than ever before under his "socially enlightened" administration. The growth of the police force over the last number of years has entailed increased aggressive intrusions into the lives of immigrant communities, people of colour, and homeless populations. In the central areas of the city especially, anti-panhandling campaigns have given the cops extensive training in criminalizing and abusing a population of people in total violation of their civil rights. In the 1930s, municipal police forces would compete with each other to try and establish the most brutal and unwelcoming regime in order to drive away and discourage the unemployed and destitute.

As homelessness in Toronto increases, an abundant supply of cops, awash in resources and highly experienced in the techniques of harassment and intimidation, will go to work on minimizing the movement of poor people in Toronto.

The particular targeting of immigrant communities is a given in just about every likely impact of the crisis that I have outlined above. OCAP frequently deals with cases of improper denial of welfare where racism appears to be a factor. Sometimes it is completely blatant. Our office dealt with a Salvadoran family who applied for medical benefits and were told by a welfare official that their claim was bogus and that he would make sure they were deported. A Somali woman applying at an Etobicoke welfare office was told that she did not need a particular benefit because she was better off in Canada than she had been in Africa. As services become increasingly restricted, we can expect this racist behaviour to become much worse. However, I suspect that we are going see more than sly, unofficial racism by public agencies. As the level of unemployment escalates, immigration authorities can be expected to increase their harassment of non-status people with US-style raids becoming a feature of daily life. We can also anticipate ugly "Canadians first" campaigns to emerge around services and employment with far right groupings working to gain influence. A powerful response to such overt displays of racist scapegoating will be vital.

The range of likely impacts and attacks on poor communities that flow from the downturn are points at which resistance can be organized. It is vital to work immediately to generate on-the-ground resistance. The work must begin with community-based organizing that defends those who face attack and abandonment. OCAP frequently uses direct action to ensure that people get the benefits that the welfare system and other bureaucracies attempt to deny them. As the unofficial imperative to deny help whenever and wherever possible moves through the welfare system, there will be a flood of cases of illegitimate denial of welfare benefits. Local committees of poor people will have to be organized to march on welfare offices and employ other militant tactics to defend people and ensure their survival.

One area of resistance that will be critical is the challenging of evictions. We must develop local networks with the capacity for rapid deployment that would make this resistance possible. A powerful and ubiquitous challenge to evictions would tilt the balance of forces, defending families in need and driving home the lesson that such attacks can be beaten back. If putting families on the street only requires sending out an official in a car to tell them to leave and to change the locks, then it's quite cost effective for the authorities. If, however, working class resistance emerges, things can change rapidly. An eviction can cease to be a bureaucratic procedure and become a major police operation that is financially and politically unwieldy. Real gains could be made in such a struggle.

The growth of homelessness will challenge a resistance movement to find means to ensure people are not just abandoned to the streets and the cops that patrol them. If shelters are overloaded and spaces in them are impossible to find, then homeless people must organize to collectively remedy such a situation. The economic crisis will likely entail the collapse of the condo boom. Condo owners will lose their homes to banks and the speculators who bought up swathes of condo units will lose their properties to the investors who financed them. The systematic movement of people into vacant condominiums is a necessary element of fighting back in the months and years ahead. This can also include takeovers of government facilities for use as additional shelter. To be sustainable, an organized resistance to the crisis must include making homes available to those who have been displaced by the interests of capital.

As communities come together to take up these kinds of fights, maintaining direct pressure at the local level is vital. As we challenge evictions on the streets, we must also demand a moratorium on evictions. "Employment insurance" must be drastically upgraded and welfare rates must be immediately restored to the spending levels that existed before the Mike Harris cuts. That means an immediate 40 percent increase in Ontario's welfare rates.

We will also need to confront the issue of "stimulation spending." If public resources are to be used for economic stimulation, the needs of communities must take precedence over the profits of corporations. Massive programs to create housing and to restore infrastructure have to be won. Those who work on such projects must do so as unionized workers and at wages that raise the general level rather than drag it down. Even some sections of the ruling class and their mouthpieces are now calling for nationalization of the banks. While it would be wrong to see this as a solution to the crisis of capitalism, to the extent that such a prospect emerges, we would need to debate and develop demands on the forms and functioning of so vital an institution as a nationalized system of allocating credit.

The task of building a resistance movement in the present situation faces some major problems. The greatest barrier to serious and effective mobilization by the working class is the labour bureaucracy that was established on the basis of the post-World War II compromise that granted concessions to unions and some improvements in social programs in return for a massive reduction in the level of working-class mobilization. During the neoliberal years, the ruling class repudiated this compromise but labour bureaucrats continued, for the most part, to respect the terms of the dead deal. Now, in conditions of fundamental crisis, the situation is even worse. Bold and decisive mobilization that goes beyond the boundaries of seeking accommodation with capitalism is the only way to make serious gains and the labour leadership is both unwilling and incapable of such action. To the contrary, they insist on taking their unions down the road of brokering and facilitating the measures of austerity that corporations say are necessary.

In the 1990s, the Ontario Labour Movement embarked on the Days of Action campaign. It showed us a glimpse of the power of the working class with its city-wide strikes and vast demonstrations, which were some of the largest in Canadian history. However, at every turn, union leaders refused to articulate that they were mobilizing to try and prevent the Harris government from proceeding with its agenda. They vacillated, unable to map out a clear plan to escalate towards a province-wide general strike and finally called off the campaign, leaving the political terrain to the Tories. The legacy of that debacle is still with us today. These dismal failings notwithstanding, the labour leadership of the mid-to-late 1990s look like radicals in comparison to how they function today.

Despite the capture of labour by an accommodationist union bureaucracy, those of us who organize in communities must realize that the power of employed workers and their organizations is a vital prerequisite for building a force that can win the battles that lie ahead. For this reason, a fight to defend communities under attack has to link up with the development of a rank-and-file challenge to the labour bureaucracy. There are already some openings to be found. A recent 85 day strike by CUPE 3903 at York University, that, against formidable odds, challenged both the underfunding of post-secondary education and the exploitation of workers within it, has shown that principled union struggles are still possible. A serious and determined campaign by activists within CUPE Ontario that led to that union taking a courageous public stand against Israeli apartheid shows that there are forces within the unions able to organize and fight outside the framework of accommodation to the status quo. The economic crisis will add to the degree to which this is true. We see the Canadian Auto Workers (CAW) union leaders beginning the process of dismantling the union's gains in their deal with General Motors. Ford and Chrysler immediately contend it is not enough. For employers, it will never be enough until CAW workers see their wages and conditions reduced to the level of the unorganized and their union is destroyed as a fighting organization and reduced to a bureaucratic shell that serves the agenda of capital. At present, perhaps understandably, 87 percent of GM workers accept concessions but, as the full extent of the "shared sacrifices" that are expected of them become clear, this will change. If the rising discontent of workers that this crisis generates can be addressed with concrete and clear proposals for a new direction for their union, a lot can be accomplished.

Outside of the labour movement, there has also been a real decline in the potential for mobilization. In the late 1980s, the Ontario Liberal Government came under great pressure and faced significant community mobilization around demands for improvements in the system of social assistance. Today, attempts by social-agency NGOs to pressure the McGuinty government to deal with poverty have been focused on a strategy of "constructive engagement" that has utilized lobbying techniques but pointedly avoided attempts to mobilize communities directly affected by poverty. In the mainstream groupings of what union bureaucrats sometimes refer to as their "social partners," we are going into this crisis with a reduced readiness to take the kinds of action that will be required if there is to be a resistance movement.

These difficulties are formidable, but we should also see that the prospects of igniting the beginnings of a movement cannot be assessed on the basis of assumptions formed prior to the onset of this crisis. We are entering a political moment in which the relative impact of correct ideas and bold action increases dramatically. In this regard, OCAP is well placed to make a significant contribution. We have gone through the difficult period along with the rest of the working class movement over the last few years. After the main challenge to the Harris Tories was demobilized, and before it could assume the scale and form that would make a victory possible, the hard-right government was replaced by a regime dedicated to the duplicitous consolidation of Harris's neoliberal Common Sense Revolution. This has been a period when there has not been a generalized upsurge but we have continued to extend our base in poor communities. The fight for the Special Diet, the drive to challenge disrepair in public housing and the struggle to rally the downtown homeless community against attempts to drive them out have strengthened that base. We are now facing a situation confronting the poor of this city that demands much more than can be put into action by OCAP alone, but the fact that a militant, anti-capitalist poor people's organization exists is a helpful factor. That we have experience in mobilizing in poor communities to win redress for individual grievances and taking up broader, direct-action based campaigns is even more promising. OCAP has provided useful examples and continues to make resources available to people as they look for ways to resist.

Efforts toward building a common front in Toronto that unites those within the anti-capitalist left who are ready to take action along non-sectarian lines is now underway. This initiative will make great gains if it can provide a lead to workers and communities facing attack. Unemployment continues to mount, people with no access to social benefits are losing their housing and workers are being told that the only way to keep their jobs is to accept austerity programs and work harder for less. That's class war and a force has to emerge that can make that war a two-sided affair. We must show that resistance can happen and that it can win. If we are to do this, it is vital that we advance an anti-capitalist perspective. This is vital because it conditions how we will organize and fight. If we accept this system, we can only look for what is possible within it. However, if we seek to defeat the system, then the needs of working class people will be fought for as non-negotiable items that are demanded regardless of the state's accounting books.

So, who will pay for this crisis? For decades now, we have been in a long retreat and most working class people have been impacted by a sense of inevitability about the agenda of capital. Resistance has been overwhelmingly defensive and, more often than not, unsuccessful. The arrogance of capitalism's ideologues has known no bounds. Thatcher lectured her victims that "there is no alternative." Fukuyama concluded that "the end of history" had arrived, so total was the victory of neoliberal capitalism in his view of things. Now the system is in crisis and, as such, it is weakened but more dangerous than ever. It is already scrambling to solve its crisis at the expense of workers and, indeed, the bulk of humanity.

But its credibility is not what it was just a few short months ago. There has been a crisis in the markets and there is a crisis in the economy but, now, there is also a crisis of legitimacy. This is a vastly changed situation in which millions of people will see the misery inflicted on them in a new light. Our immediate capacity to exploit it is less than what we would hope but the speed by which we can change is a practical organizational challenge we need to take up without delay.

There has been a crisis brewing long before the subprime mortgages made the situation immanent. People are angry and know that things are going from bad to worse. This is becoming a generalized working class experience. People need practical proof that these worsening conditions are neither inevitable nor unstoppable. This is the starting point for a resistance movement with a bold anti-capitalist vision of what that movement must fight for. Of necessity, we respond to this crisis with working class resistance to any and all attempts to stabilize the system at our expense. However, we must fight back in such a way as to expose the impossibility of continuing with a society that applies its vast productive power on the basis of the profit needs of a small social class. To fail to recognize this is to accept inequality, poverty, and worsening crises. Our struggles can't be limited to the goal of attaining what rights we can under capitalism. A society based on collective ownership and democratic political and economic decision making is the only means to solve this crisis and create a world where human needs are met and the human personality is developed to its full potential. ★

4STRUGGLEMAG

an ongoing zine, edited by anti-imperialist
political prisoner, Jaan Laaman

from the hearts and minds of north american
political prisoners and their friends

4strugglemag.org

P.O. Box 42053 Succ. Jeanne Mance, Montreal QC, H2W 2T3

Knowing the Terrain

BDS in the Wake of the Gaza Onslaught

Shourideh Molavi

In a cartoon by Brazillian artist Carlos Latuff an Israeli Apache helicopter fires a rocket directly at a Palestinian child. Wearing a kaffaiyah and holding a teddy bear, the child stands alone, the word "Gaza" narrowing at his bare feet. A concrete wall with watchtowers marks the horizon, and the Israeli attack chopper dominates a blood red sky. Used to promote this year's Israeli Apartheid Week, Latuff's cartoon captures the political and humanitarian realities of Israel's "Operation Cast Lead," the most destructive and violent act of military aggression Israel has carried out against Palestinians since the Second Intifada.

The 22-day onslaught in Gaza raised the international profile of the plight of the Palestinian people and inspired a massive outburst of global solidarity. Millions of people around the world expressed their outrage through mass demonstrations, sit-ins, occupations, writing campaigns, media statements, and various other actions.[1] In many places, the size and composition of the demonstrations helped to place the 61-year Palestinian struggle for self-determination at the forefront of broader anti-war mobilizations.

Renewed attention to the conflict compelled a growing number of individuals and groups to join the campaign for Boycott, Divestment, and Sanctions (BDS) against Israel, a campaign launched in 2005 by over 170 Palestinian organizations.[2] Many of these newly activated individuals and groups specifically cited the Gaza massacre as their motivation for joining the campaign and openly condemned the operation for what it was: a war crime. With this unprecedented global response to the massacres in Gaza, solidarity activists must consider how to respond to situations in which massacres halfway around the world become the focus of political and social attention "at home."

There's no doubt that the horror of the Gaza onslaught created new openings for organizing. Prominent individuals and groups were compelled to affirm their support for the Palestinian struggle, and movement newcomers were able to plug into an existing solidarity movement that has been working closely with Palestinian civil society organizations and community representatives. However, the BDS movement cannot simply be satisfied with increasing its global support base. The movement must maintain its focus on dismantling Zionism by making it difficult and costly for complicit governments and institutions at home to support Israel's apartheid system.

As part of this focus, solidarity activists must clarify what constitutes effective political support for the Palestinian cause. Developments at home, however significant for the BDS movement, do not necessarily translate into a transformation of the conditions imposed on Palestinians under Israel's oppressive military system. Solidarity groups should embrace the current global growth in the BDS movement with a sober awareness of the continuing political realities facing Palestinians. Real success means lasting political and social transformation on the ground for Palestinians living in Gaza, the West Bank, inside Israel, and in the refugee camps of the region. Political changes at home that have allowed for the growth of the BDS movement must be nurtured and expanded, but they should not be mistaken for real success.

A "New" Political Reality?

The Gaza war of 2009 marks a bloody new chapter in Palestinian and regional history. In this way, its political and moral effects are comparable to those of the Sabra and Shatila massacre of 1982, when the ultra-nationalist Lebanese Phalangist militia slaughtered over 3,000 Palestinian men, women, and children in the Sabra and Shatila refugee camps, which for three horrifying nights were lit up by flares fired by the surrounding Israeli army.

Prior to the 1982 Israeli invasion of southern Lebanon and the siege of Beirut, the Lebanese people had been fighting a devastating civil war involving many local and global political players and funders. With the Israeli ground and air forces' invasion, however, Lebanon suffered more death and devastation in three months than it had during the preceding seven years. The Sabra and Shatila massacres that took place under the watchful eye of the Israeli military were a dramatic and terrible reminder of the intersection of internal Lebanese political problems with the Israeli-Palestinian conflict.

This devastating legacy irrevocably exposed the historical and contemporary crisis of Palestinian refugees. Victims of Zionist ethnic cleansing campaigns in 1948, of dehumanizing domestic policies in Lebanon, and of Israel's military aggression, the plight of Palestinian refugees came to the fore of discourse around the conflict. The larger context of Palestinian expulsion and dispossession was permanently inscribed on the platform of solidarity movements around the world.

Similar to Sabra and Shatila, the latest Gaza onslaught is the product of an intersection of the inter-Palestinian power struggle, the failure of Arab unity, geopolitical conflict with Iran, internal Israeli politics, and the broader Israeli-Palestinian conflict. The war has given its devastated survivors a new role and identity on the world stage as engaged actors rather than passive victims on the receiving end of perpetual Israeli aggression. Their narratives, testimonies and documentation of the appalling and illegal conduct of the Israeli army during Operation Cast Lead have shaped new public understanding and discourses about the conflict. As in Latuff's cartoon, the world's attention has focused again at the feet of the Palestinian men, women and children trapped in the besieged Strip, showered with missiles and white phosphorous.

It Started in Gaza

A close look at the history of the Palestinian national self-determination movement reveals that the fate of Gaza mirrors the conflict as a whole. The creation of the state of Israel in May 1948 and the subsequent partition of Palestine radically increased the population of Gaza from just below 100,000 to nearly 300,000 people, due to the influx of refugees, most of whom were fleeing Zionist forces that had invaded the Jaffa area and the Negev.[3] After 1948, Gaza came under Egyptian rule and Jordon controlled the West Bank, thus marking the beginning of Palestine's division into two separate territorial entities.

This remained the case until Israel, with French and British cooperation, reoccupied the Strip in the October 1956 Suez War, after which pressure from the United States and the international community soon forced a withdrawal. Gaza was returned to Egypt in 1957, only to be occupied again by Israel in 1967. The bilateral peace agreement brokered between Israeli Prime Minister Menachem Begin and Egyptian President Anwar Sadat at Camp David in 1978 returned the Sinai peninsula to Egypt. This agreement caused ripples throughout the Middle East, setting a despicable precedent for peace-packages offered to other Arab states: normalize relations with Israel in exchange for the return of occupied or annexed land while sacrificing a just solution for Palestinians.

Although United Nations Resolution 242 called for negotiations leading to Israeli withdrawal from lands occupied in the 1967 war, the resolution has yet to provide tangible results. For 38 years, the military occupation remained unchanged and the Israeli government undertook various measures to strengthen its presence in Gaza, the most disastrous of which was the confiscation of large amounts of land on which to build Jewish-only settlements. The effects of the Israeli occupation – a debilitated economy and a large poverty-stricken refugee population – soon made the Strip a centre of Palestinian political unrest and activism. Gaza was the site of numerous demonstrations, widespread riots, and violent confrontations between the Israeli army and Palestinian resisters. Beginning in the Jabalia refugee camp in northern Gaza on December 9, 1987, and quickly spreading to Jerusalem and the rest of the Palestinian territories, these actions developed into the first Intifada, a historic turning point in the conflict that effectively put the Palestinian struggle on the global political map.

The first Intifada led to the 1993 Oslo Accords and the signing of the Declaration of Principles between Israel and the Palestine Liberation Organization. Oslo I (which was expanded in 1995 with Oslo II to include additional towns and cities) provided for limited Palestinian self-rule in the form of the Palestinian Authority (PA). Gaza was designated a testing ground for Palestinian self-rule. Despite the presence of PA forces, however, Israel has maintained control over Gaza to this day. Even after implementing its unilateral Disengagement Plan in September 2005, Israel controls air space, entry and exit points for goods and people, territorial waters, maritime access, the population registry, and the tax system.

Former Israeli Prime Minister Ariel Sharon first announced the unilateral Disengagement Plan in his address to the Fourth

Herzliya conference in December 2003, promoting the notion that "separation from the Palestinians was the only solution to preserve a Jewish and democratic Israeli state." In proposing the unilateral withdrawal and evacuation of Israeli settlers from Gaza, Sharon stressed that Israel would never cede Jerusalem and the West Bank. Rather than a complete withdrawal from all occupied Palestinian lands, the measure allotted paltry powers to the PA. Praised by the governments of Canada, the US, Europe, and the United Nations, the so-called disengagement allowed Israel to disavow legal and political responsibility for the 1.5 million Palestinians living in Gaza, while continuing to exercise exclusive control over the population. In Gaza, the Israeli leadership experimented with continuously expanding and consolidating control, all the while ridding themselves of responsibilities under the provisions of the Geneva Conventions and Hague Regulations concerning occupied territories. Such experimentation will likely be the model for any future "withdrawal" from the Bantustans of the West Bank, as Israel continues to devise means by which to ensure its demographic aims of having a Jewish majority occupy as much Palestinian land as possible.

January 2006 elections confirmed the strength of the Hamas movement in Gaza (where it emerged in 1988), although it also made significant strides in the West Bank. When Israel and Western powers demanded that the newly elected Hamas government renounce violence, recognize the Jewish state, and promise to abide by past peace agreements, its leaders only went as far as withdrawing its call for the destruction of Israel from its election manifesto, agitating instead for the establishment of "an independent state whose capital is Jerusalem." The imposition of international sanctions against the Strip followed, along with a suspension of foreign aid to the PA and the transfer of Palestinian taxes, causing unprecedented stagnation within the Palestinian economy, particularly in Gaza. Leaders in Fatah and Hamas turned on each other, and, as attempts at a national unity government stalled, the 2007 "battle of Gaza" ensued. The success of Hamas in securing control of the Strip demonstrates its strength and likely its long-term presence on the political scene. Indeed, March 2008 polls indicated the continued popularity of Hamas with "more respondents naming the administration of Ismail Haniyeh as the legitimate government than that of Fatah's Salam Fayyad."[4]

We cannot underestimate the importance of the Gaza Strip for understanding this conflict. Gaza is the historic site of major political and social turns in the Palestinian national movement, all of which provide observers with insights into the tactics the State of Israel uses to pursue its ideological, territorial, and political interests in the region. A close inspection of the latest onslaught in Gaza provides important insights into recent regional and geopolitical developments.

Organized Genocide

Operation Cast Lead, launched in Gaza at 11:30 a.m. on December 27, 2008, resulted in massive civilian casualties. The Israeli army used extreme force, shelling densely populated civilian neighborhoods, buildings, media centres, mosques, schools, and UN relief convoys. The casualties reached immense proportions: more than 1,400 people were killed and more than 5,000 were injured in just three weeks. Arabic media operating inside Gaza released sickening images of mass suffering, dismembered bodies, and widespread destruction. Stories rapidly surfaced of entire families buried under the rubble of their bombed houses. Starving children were found sitting next to their dead parents. One-and-a-half million Gazans were held hostage to what John Ging, the head of the United Nation's Relief and Works Agency in the Gaza Strip, called "a full blown humanitarian crisis."5 Against the backdrop of a UN-sponsored school in Jabaliya refugee camp that was reduced to flaming rubble, the surrounding streets stained by the blood of at least 42 Palestinians, most of them children, Ging stated: "There is nowhere safe in Gaza. Everyone here is terrorized and traumatized."

The global community quickly understood what voices on the ground asserted on the first day of the attacks: there can be no such thing as "surgical operations" in Gaza. In such a congested and densely populated area, civilians are indistinguishable from so-called military targets. Indeed, Hamas' entire record of damage to Israel is minor when measured against what Israel managed to inflict in the first few minutes of the Gaza blitzkrieg. Millions of outraged people around the world staged actions, issued public statements, launched letter writing campaigns, and signed petitions. They took their disgust with the brutal onslaught to the streets, demanding that their governments exert political pressure on Israel.

International organizations and prominent human rights figures also launched scathing criticisms. During the onslaught, the president of the United Nations General Assembly, Miguel d'Escoto Brockmann, accused Israel of violating international law, telling an emergency session of the UN General Assembly in New York that "Gaza is ablaze. It has been turned into a burning hell."[6] Based on preliminary evidence collected after the military invasion, Richard Falk, the UN Special Rapporteur on Human Rights in the Palestinian territories, concluded that Israel's actions "seem to constitute a war crime of the greatest magnitude under international law."[7] Most recently, in an open letter to UN Secretary General Ban Ki-Moon and the UN Security Council, leading human rights figures – including Nobel Laureate Archbishop Desmond Tutu and Richard Goldstone, a former chief prosecutor in Yugoslavia and Rwanda – called for the UN to launch a war crimes inquiry.[8]

As part of a growing movement, prominent Jewish figures and human rights groups issued profound condemnations. Senior member of the British Parliament's Labour Party, Gerald Kaufman, and Holocaust survivor and senior academic, Hajo Meyer, compared some Israeli actions to those of the Nazis.[9] The International Jewish Anti-Zionist Network echoed this comparison on this year's Holocaust Remembrance Day. In a letter to *The Guardian*, renowned Jewish British intellectuals and professionals compared Gaza to the Warsaw Ghetto, demanding that their government "withdraw the British ambassador to Israel and, as with apartheid South Africa, embark on a programme of boycott, divestment and sanctions."[10]

Exposing the Mirage

Deep political and ideological rifts within the Arab world surfaced during the Gaza onslaught. Observers of the incursion witnessed a "battle of summits" between the Qatari-Syrian and Saudi-Egyptian camps, often referred to as an "Arab cold war". By annoucing their willingness to cut diplomatic and economic relations, the Qatari-Syrian group adopted a stronger ideological stance against the Israeli occupation and recognized the need to address final status issues and include Hamas in political process. In contrast, seeking to secure its own leadership in the Arab world, the Saudi-Egyptian camp opted to micromanage the occupation, neglecting broader political questions and instead focus on rebuilding Gaza on Israeli and American terms. The platform of this so-called moderate Arab camp is well-suited to American and Israeli interests: it seeks to impose limited pressure on Israel while ensuring that Hamas will come to depend on Egypt's goodwill, thereby distancing Hamas from its Iranian backers. As Egyptian President Hosni Mubarak stated, "whoever wants to contribute and also see the fruits of his contribution will have to pass through Cairo or through the Palestinian Authority in Ramallah."

At the same time, Middle Eastern governments of all stripes have banned demonstrations against Israeli actions in Gaza and their security forces have beaten and arrested demonstrators. It is generally acknowledged that the rights to peaceful assembly, dissent, and free expression are severely curtailed in the region: Human Rights Watch reports that Egypt has been under an emergency law for 27 years that allows authorities to prohibit demonstrations; Saudi Arabia has no law regulating assembly and any political demonstrations can be banned by executive orders; while Jordan routinely denies permission for demonstrations that involve criticism of the country's domestic or foreign policy.[11] What is less recognized is that these prohibitions apply even when dissent is directed against Israeli war crimes.

Human Rights Watch reports that on December 30, 2008, the Saudi Ministry of the Interior denied permission to a group of Saudi activists seeking to organize a demonstration against Israel's attacks. Two days later in Riyadh, authorities arrested two human rights activists who had arrived despite the ban. In the Eastern Province, another Saudi group organized demonstrations against the Gaza blockade on December 19 and against the military operation on December 29. At both actions, Saudi security forces arrested at least 23 people, and continue to detain and torture one of the demonstrators, Kamil al-Ahmad, who refused to sign a pledge not to demonstrate again.[12]

A similar pattern emerged in Jordan and Egypt. Just over a week into the Gaza onslaught, demonstrators in Jordan (including Al Jazeera Arabic satellite television bureau chief Yasir Abu Hilala) gathered in front of the Israeli embassy and were greeted by riot police, beaten, and arrested. In Egypt, the Muslim Brotherhood reported arrests of almost 900 of its members in connection with demonstrations protesting Israeli actions in Gaza.[13] The 15,000 participants in a January 16 demonstration north of Cairo faced police brutality and numerous arrests. Dissenters in Egypt have even been denied the right to criticize Israel online. Egypt has arrested bloggers and activists for expressions of organized solidarity with the people of Gaza. As Sarah Leah Whitson of Human Rights Watch notes, "Apparently it's not enough for the

Egyptian government to imprison its own critics; it is now intent on silencing Egyptians who criticize Israel as well."[14]

Contrary to popular assumptions, similarly repressive tactics have been employed against independent criticism of Israel in the Iranian Republic. Iranian President Mahmoud Ahmadinejad's denunciation of Arab passivity in the face of a "rare genocide" echoed on the Arab street, as did demands for economic and diplomatic pressure on Israel as a minimum recourse. Ahmadinejad's sharp criticisms of the Zionist attacks in Gaza provoked a surge in the popularity of the Iranian leader throughout the Arab world. Indeed, it is pro-Iranian sentiment that has prompted the Arab alliance of so-called "moderates" – Egypt, Saudi Arabia, Jordan, and the PA – to toe the line against Hamas. But while the Iranian regime is capable of staunch verbal condemnations of Israeli war crimes, it only tolerates official government-sponsored expressions of solidarity with the Palestinian people. For instance, on January 11, Iranian plain-clothes security agents violently dispersed a gathering convened in front of the Palestinian embassy in Tehran. Although the protest, organized by an independent Iranian group called Mothers for Peace, was held to oppose the violence in the Gaza Strip, Iranian security forces beat and arrested numerous demonstrators, imposing restrictions on non-governmental forms of dissent against Israel.[15]

This pattern of repression reveals that regional governments use criticism of Israel and solidarity with the people of Gaza as political tools to bolster their domestic authority. Existing regimes exploit Gazan suffering to reinforce their own political rule. As a result, only official government-sanctioned demonstrations are tolerated, while the rights of political opponents – even those mirroring the states' political positions – are brutally denied. Indeed, as Whitson notes, "Middle Eastern regimes are throwing one symbolic shoe at Israel while using the other shoe to strike at domestic dissent."

Not even the West Bank is immune to this pattern. The Palestinian Authority and Israeli forces collaborated to impose serious restrictions on organized dissent in the West Bank. According to Al Jazeera Arabic, the PA banned pro-Hamas demonstrations in the West Bank shortly after Israel started its attacks on Gaza. PA officials arrested demonstrators in Ramallah for waving Hamas flags, clashed with student protesters at Bir Zeit University, and fired tear gas to disperse large crowds. Meanwhile, the Israeli military in the West Bank injured protesters in violent clashes after banning peaceful demonstrations.[16] This repression, part and parcel of the firming up of Israeli support for the Palestinian Prime Minster Mahmoud Abbas, successfully delegitimized the Fatah party on the Palestinian street and has turned Abbas into a political corpse. As a result, Fatah's fate has diverged from that of Hamas; it is no longer the case that Hamas' loss will necessarily be Fatah's gain.

International Complicity

Unrelenting American support for Israel is nothing new, and it should come as no surprise that then president-elect Barak Obama was aware and supportive of the Israeli onslaught. In an interview with the French Al-Ahram daily newspaper in late February, US intellectual Noam Chomsky outlined the "premeditated plan" behind the brutal military invasion. Chomsky notes that the plan was to "deliver the maximum blow to Gaza before the new US president took office, so that he could put these matters behind him." Operation Cast Lead was intended to ease Obama's pledge to settle the Israeli-Palestinian conflict by creating a "new security reality" in Gaza, significantly damaging Hamas' standing army and giving its leadership a clear sense of the threat to their rule. Obama attempted to justify his silence about Israel's incursion with the claim that "there is only one president at a time," but, as Chomsky points out, Obama issued statements after the Mumbai bombings and made various moves in the economic sphere while still president-elect. Further, Obama's repeated assertion that "defending Israel is a US priority" indicates that existing US policy on the Palestinian question will continue.

The stark pro-Israeli outlook of the Canadian government was similarly evident during the attack on Gaza. Hoping to stay silent, Prime Minister Stephen Harper did not issue a statement until two-weeks into the launch of the Israeli air and ground attacks. Given the backlash he faced over his previous claim that Israel's devastating military attack on Lebanon in 2006 was a "measured" response, Harper steered clear of details and merely called for a "durable" ceasefire by both parties. Peter Kent, Canada's junior foreign affairs minister, was more honest about the government's position when he placed the burden of responsibility squarely at Hamas' feet, stating that "Canada has, since the election of this [Hamas] government, been quite clear in supporting Israel's right to defend itself."[17] Although shameful, this should not come as a surprise.

Canada's support of Israel is abundantly clear, particularly in the accelerated integration of Canadian and Israeli security, academic, military, industrial, and corporate establishments in the fields of public safety, riot control, emergency preparedness, homeland security, immigration, trade, aerospace and marine technology, and cyber-based privacy and communications technology.

Whatever integrity the United Nations and its associated institutions still had after the US-led wars on Afghanistan and Iraq dissolved with the Gaza blitzkrieg. UN General Assembly President Brockmann conveyed his disgust with Israel's record of violations, noting:

> It seems to me ironic that Israel, a State that, more than any other, owes its very existence to a General Assembly resolution, should be so disdainful of United Nations' resolutions. Prime Minister Olmert's recent statement disavowing the authority of Security Council Resolution 1860 clearly places Israel as a State in contempt of international law and the United Nations.[18]

Brockmann also pointed out the dysfunctionality of the United Nations, condemning international complicity in the plight of the Palestinian people:

> But there is still another violation – one in which we, as the United Nations, are directly complicit. The blockade of Gaza, which has now been going on for 19 months, has been directly responsible for the widespread humanitarian crisis in Gaza even before the current Israeli assault began.... Yet the blockade has been endorsed, at least tacitly, by powerful parties grouped in the Quartet, placing this Organization in a dubious role and in violation of our obligations under the Charter and international law.

Israel ignored the Security Council's resolution that called for an immediate, durable, and fully respected ceasefire, and the war on Gaza began as it ended: unilaterally. The high number of Palestinian deaths, vast destruction of infrastructure and residential areas, apparently indiscriminate attacks, and the use of experimental weapons provoked accusations regarding the legality of the military operation. Luis Moreno Ocampo, chief prosecutor of the International Criminal Court, has received over 200 appeals from Palestinian, Israeli, and international NGOs urging investigation into the attacks in Gaza.

Israel is now well aware of the legal challenges it faces. In addition to keeping its officers tight-lipped about the details of the onslaught, the Israeli Defense Ministry issued new regulations strengthening censorship rules to prevent more detailed reporting or the disclosure of the identities of officers. As *Ha'aretz* journalist Yotam Feldman reports, there was an unprecedented level of participation by Israeli experts in international humanitarian law during the Gaza onslaught. Feldman outlines the resolve of the International Law Division of the Israeli Military's Advocate General's Office to "adopt the most flexible interpretations of the law in order to justify IDF operations."

The Gaza operation provoked a growing recognition of the pressing need for reconsideration of existing political approaches to dealing with the Palestinian leadership. The inclusion of Hamas in political and diplomatic venues is necessary for the establishment of parameters of engagement that might allow for a lasting and just solution. The continued isolation of the democratically elected government in Gaza is devastating to Palestinians: it limits efforts at national reconciliation; prevents a unity government between Fatah and Hamas; maintains the existing organized starvation and oppression of the besieged Palestinians; and grants Israel carte blanche in its military and political confrontations with the Hamas government, and by extension, the Gazan population as a whole.

The True Face of Israeli Democracy

The military incursion into Gaza was accompanied by violent crackdowns on Palestinian-Arab dissenters inside Israel. During the war in Gaza, Israeli police arrested 763 demonstrators inside Israel, most of whom were Arab, for what Israeli police spokesperson Mickey Rosenfield called "violent disturbances." In addition, dozens of Arabs were rounded up to be "warned ahead of time not to cause trouble, and then released." Recent protests by Arab citizens of Israel have been larger and more frequent, and are quickly and sometimes aggressively broken up.[19]

Political and legal repression has also intensified. An Israeli Parliamentary Elections Committee moved to disqualify two Arab-led political parties, the Balad Party and the United Arab List, from the national Israeli elections that were held in February. The motion – which was supported by Israeli parties across the political spectrum – sought to charge the two groups with "disloyalty" for their strong criticisms of the war on Gaza under a law passed in

2002 permitting the exclusion of political factions supporting "armed struggle by a terrorist organization or foreign country."[20]

Calls for disqualification pointed to the Arab-led parties' demands that Israel be a "state for all its citizens" rather than a legally inscribed "Jewish state." The discourse of equal citizenship in a bi-national state is growing in popularity with the Arab community inside Israel. Their unique situation – as citizens of Israel and members of the Palestinian nation – has been largely unaddressed in previous negotiations. The organized sectors of this Palestinian community issued three major documents in 2007 outlining their vision of an equal and bi-national Israeli state: the Haifa Declaration, the Democratic Constitution, and the Future Vision.[21] The three documents call for a bi-national Israel, a proposal that translates into an existential nightmare for the majority of the Israeli population. In fact, during her recent election campaign to become Israel's prime minister, then Foreign Minister Tzipi Livni indicated that the formation of a Palestinian state in the West Bank and Gaza Strip would provide "a national solution" that would allow the Israeli establishment to tell the Arab community within Israel that their "national aspirations lie elsewhere."[22]

Overall, the war in Gaza remobilized the Arab population inside Israel to a degree not seen since the second Intifada. The political ramifications of the war for this community were so stark that, rather than approaching the Israeli government, groups in the Arab community inside Israel approached the Hamas government to free Palestinian prisoners who are citizens of Israel.[23]

Effective Solidarity

As it stands, effective solidarity with the Palestinian people must go beyond demands for a temporary ceasefire or a truce between Israel and Hamas. Solidarity work needs to address Israeli war crimes and demand equal citizenship for Arabs in Israel, the right of return for refugees, a lift of the siege on Gaza, and an end to the illegal and brutal military occupation and exploitation of Palestinian lands and labour. Such action requires a determined, organized, and long-term push to put into action the 2005 call for BDS, which outlines Palestinian expectations of international solidarity groups. Palestinian solidarity activists must renew the drive towards the organized isolation of all Israeli institutions, corporations, and government representatives, all of whom are complicit in its apartheid system.

The recent successes of BDS work after the Gaza onslaught have not gone unnoticed by the Israeli government. In response to the growing Palestine solidarity movement, particularly in Canada, the Israeli foreign ministry has introduced its "Brand Israel" campaign, a 10-month-long $4-million initiative launched in Toronto, with political and financial support from established Canadian business and political leaders. The campaign seeks to direct public attention away from Israel's brutal military occupation and towards its "medical and technological developments... cultural acts and scientific achievements... [and its] film, food and wine festivals featuring Israel-made products."[24] However, the massacres in Gaza during the latest 22-day onslaught make this next to impossible. Unfortunately for its apologists, images of Israel's organized slaughter of an oppressed people have outraged and mobilized popular forces around the world, foregrounding the Palestinian cause.

The Israeli attack on the Gaza Strip has given this movement a powerful motive to redouble its efforts. Dozens of existing BDS efforts have gained momentum and publicity while many new campaigns were set in motion during or immediately after the onslaught. The weak official positions and declarations of governments stood in stark contrast to the outbursts of rage in streets across the globe. However, this recent wave of protests has a particular characteristic differentiating it from past mobilizations: energy and outrage is being channelled into effective grassroots political action, mainly in the form of the ongoing BDS campaign. The tangible advances BDS activism made immediately after the attack on Gaza are a direct result of many years of underacknowledged organizing, networking, and mobilizing initiated after the 2005 call to action. The task for activists now is to channel popular outrage into coordinated, collective action.

Activists should move beyond hand-wringing about the efficacy of BDS and begin to organize and mobilize the growing numbers of individuals and groups who, while outraged and focused on the events in Gaza, have yet to connect with the BDS movement. The world's explicit focus on the slaughter of people living in a tiny, devastated strip of land halfway across the world provides such an opportunity. In this context, effective solidarity requires that activists identify the connections between massacres overseas, local complicity, and possible opportunities for political change. ★

Notes

1   www.europe-solidaire.org/spip.php?article12631

2   www.bdsmovement.net/?q=/glob

3   www.passia.org/publications/bulletins/gaza/index.htm

4   Ibid.

5   http://thescotsman.scotsman.com/latestnews/Gaza-A-39fullblown-humanitarian-crisis39.4849313.jp

6   http://english.aljazeera.net/news/americas/2009/01/2009115171631306757.html

7   http://news.yahoo.com/s/nm/20090320/wl_nm/us_israel_palestinians_crimes

8   www.telegraph.co.uk/news/worldnews/middleeast/israel/4998082/Desmond-Tutu-demands-Gaza-war-crimes-inquiry.html

9   http://jta.org/news/article/2009/01/16/1002308/mp-kaufman-likens-israelis-to-nazis,%20

10 www.guardian.co.uk/world/2009/jan/10/letters-gaza-uk

11 www.unhcr.org/refworld/country,,,,SAU,4562d8cf2,4978449fc,0.html

12 Ibid.

13 Ibid.

14 www.hrw.org/en/news/2009/03/04/egypt-hundreds-still-held-over-gaza-protests

15 http://www.unhcr.org/refworld/country,,,,SAU,4562d8cf2,4978449fc,0.html

16 www.unhcr.org/refworld/country,,,,SAU,4562d8cf2,4978449fc,0.html

17 www.peterkent.ca/EN/8128/79314

18 http://un.org/ga/president/63/statements/onpalestine15019.shtml

19 www.washingtonpost.com/wp-dyn/content/article/2009/01/19/AR2009011902608_2.html?sid=ST2009011903126

20 Ibid.

21 Haifa Declaration: www.mada-research.org/archive/haifaenglish.pdf, Democratic Constitution: www.adalah.org/eng/constitution.php, and Future Vision Document: www.mossawacenter.org/files/files/File/Reports/2006/future%20Vision%20(English).pdf

22 www.cbn.com/CBNnews/500388.aspx

23 www.ynet.co.il/english/articles/0,7340,L-3686784,00.html

24 www.thestar.com/News/GTA/article/346848

turbulence
ideas for movement

Online and in print
www.turbulence.org.uk

"They're Clear-Cutting Our Way of Life"

Algonquins Defend the Forest

Shiri Pasternak[1]

One of the most dangerous First Nations in Canada is a small community of around 250 Algonquins living in rural Québec. The threat they pose is so grave that the Canadian government has repeatedly intervened in their customary governance laws to put minority community factions in power. The Mitchikanibikok Inik, or Algonquins of Barriere Lake (ABL), have not taken up arms, nor do they occupy land near major transport arteries like Highway 401 that could be disrupted to costly economic effect. The danger posed by the ABL lies with a "Trilateral Agreement," a co-management plan signed in the early 1990s that covers governance over the land, wildlife, and resources on 10,000 square kilometers of their unsurrendered traditional territory.

To understand the nature of this "menace," some knowledge of the current land claims process is required. Canada's preferred land claims negotiation process forces First Nations to extinguish their Aboriginal rights and title upon settlement, to give up communal land rights for "fee simple" (private property) ownership, and to shoulder costly legal and land-use mapping costs that eventually get docked from meager settlements. The government can withdraw at any time from the bargaining process. The ABL rejected this land claims approach and they have been paying the price in their community ever since.

In 1991, Canada and Québec agreed to the Trilateral Agreement which is a landmark conservation plan. Since then, the Algonquins have been fighting to have it implemented. Implementing the Agreement would ensure that they had a decisive voice in resource management decisions on their territory, the protection of traditional Algonquin land uses, and modest revenue-sharing deals – in addition to financing extensive and sophisticated traditional land use maps. The Trilateral Agreement sets a vital precedent that the government is determined to reverse. Signed during the heady days of co-operative federalism, with the shadow of Oka cast over Indian Country, negotiating the Trilateral proved to be a mistake the government would come to sorely regret.

The Canadian federal government and the Québec provincial government have clearly decided that the Trilateral Agreement, which provides a viable alternative to their preferred land claims process, must be stopped at any cost, even if that includes tear-gassing elders and children and arresting community leaders at non-violent road blockades.

The roots of the struggle lie in the Algonquins' traditional ways of life, nurtured and transmitted from one generation to the next. There are few hunting societies left within the Ottawa-Montréal boreal region and the Algonquins proudly maintain their cultural survival by relying upon these traditional practices. Take, for example, the ABL's school calendar: for two weeks each fall and spring the school closes for "beaver break"; an opportunity to teach the children about trapping and to get them out onto the land. Rare among the Algonquin nation, the entire Barriere Lake community can claim Algonquin, and not French or English, as their first language.

Despite the cultural richness of the community, the poverty on the reserve is dire. An estimated $100 million is extracted from their traditional territory annually in logging, hydro, and sport fishing/hunting revenues, but the Algonquins don't see a dime of it. Most of the community lives on social assistance, much of their housing has been condemned by Health Canada, and the diesel generator that electrifies the tiny fifty-nine-acre reserve is barely able to keep up with demand.

The recent history of the ABL's struggle for the Trilateral Agreement provides an important lesson on the perils of the path away from colonial land claim negotiations. In this case, a viable alternative co-management model for nation to nation negotiations would mean a real transfer of power over lucrative resource extraction by powerful corporations and states to a tiny and financially impoverished indigenous community. The Trilateral Agreement represents the commitment to respectful relations between nations that the wampums signify. This relationship has never been forgotten by the ABL, as was simply and powerfully displayed on a recent blockade banner: "Honour Your Word."

Early History

Since time immemorial, the ABL have occupied over 44,000 kms of land in what is now the Outouais region of Québec, about 300 kilometers north of Ottawa. The Barriere Lake traditional land use area reaches from the northern Gatineau River and the headwaters of the Ottawa River southwest across the present Cabonga Reservoir to the Coulonge River.

The ABL are one of ten present-day Algonquin communities in the Ottawa River watershed that straddle the Québec–Ontario border. As their name and surrounding band names suggest, Algonquin territorial organization and land management is based on watersheds and waterways serving as boundaries for family, band, and tribal territories. The ABL once traveled extensively along these watery highways, spending their winters in the bush in extended families, hunting large game like moose and deer, and trapping fur-bearing animals, particularly beaver, which were of critical socio-economic and cultural significance. Though soil conditions were poorly suited to agricultural production, the community lived relatively well by hunting, fishing, trapping, gathering plant foods and harvesting traditional medicines.

The gradual displacement and dispossession of the ABL from their traditional territory has taken place over several centuries, by means of mounting restrictions and encroachments aimed at replacing their indigenous system of land tenure and jurisdiction with the laws and regulations of settler society.

In the early history of contact, the fur trade governed relations between the Algonquin, the French, and other settlers. Permanent European settlement in the territory began in the 1830s, when logging replaced the fur trade as the main economic activity. With logging came incursions by white settlers who hunted and trapped indiscriminately, decimating wildlife populations. By the 1870s, most of the ABL's traditional territory was leased out to timber companies. From 1870-1913 an incredible 59 percent of Québec's revenue from timber came from the two regions that make up the ABL's traditional territory.

While the federal government did attempt to intervene on the ABL's behalf, provincial policy flouted federal interventions and failed to even acknowledge the presence of the Algonquin people in the region. In 1929, several ABL community members drowned when a river unexpectedly overflowed – no one had bothered to inform them that the Gatineau Paper Company, a subsidiary of Canadian International Paper (CIP), was constructing dams to form a reservoir 100 square miles wide on their territory. The community was forced to relocate their settlement. A few years later and further south, CIP constructed more dams to provide power to their mills, this time flooding an additional 150 square miles of land in the heart of the ABL's traditional territory.

Even bigger changes were to come in 1938 with the construction of the Mont-Laurier – Senneterre highway (now highway 117), which opened the region for tourism and sport-hunting purposes. Fiercely independent, the ABL pushed deeper into the forest, banned as they were from the 10-mile corridor created on either side of the highway for tourist recreation, where hunting and trapping were forbidden to the Algonquins.

Throughout the late 1940s, the Algonquins refused to abide by restrictive laws mandating permits for hunting and trapping. They further refused to be searched for "illegal" beaver pelts by police authorities after trapping had been banned and refused to make maps of their hunting territory or to provide demographic data for government collection.

In 1950, La Vérendrye Wildlife Reserve was established on ABL territory, creating new jurisdictional conflicts. Around this period, the ABL came to rely on a mixed economy to supplement their traditional livelihood, engaging in waged labour employment that included trapping, seasonal work at fur farms in the US, cutting trees for CIP, and guiding moose hunters. Ten years after their territory was unilaterally turned into a park, Québec finally transferred some land to the federal government to establish a Reserve for the Barriere Lake Algonquins at Rapid Lake. The ABL had been petitioning for land since 1876. But the reserve introduced a new slate of problems. They were given a measly 59-acre plot of eroded and sandy land totally insufficient for a few hundred people – no core infrastructure was built, no community development plan was established, and severe wildlife scarcities ensued.

The government believed the reserve land at Rapid Lake would silence complaints and satisfy local native land claims. However, the ABL never considered the reserve as a settlement of their land claims, but simply as lands set aside from settler excursion. This understanding is embedded in the Algonquin name for the reserve, "Kitiganik," which translates roughly to mean "place to be planted"; the Algonquin saw themselves as planted there by the government, and did not intend to stay there permanently.

The ABL had other reasons to believe that their land would be protected. The Algonquins are signatories to the Treaty of Niagara of 1764, which ensured that no native lands could be sold before being ceded to the Crown by First Nations. The ABL never ceded their land. The Royal Proclamation of 1763 issued by King George III had also ensured such provisions, which remain enshrined in Section 35 of the 1982 Canadian Constitution.

The Barriere Lake Algonquins' three-figure wampum belt, which dates back to the 1760s, provides further evidence of an agreement between the community, the Church, and the settlers. The belt depicts an understanding whereby, under the sign of the cross, no interference would be made into the local native ways of life. Woven into hair pins and stamped onto letterheads, the wampum has endured to this day as a symbol of an agreement between nations.

In 1970, at a meeting with government officials, elder Paul Matchewan said: "The moose, the birds and the fish, things by which our people lived, are being slaughtered by licensed hunters from outside. The government derives the benefit." Four years later, the Barriere Lake Algonquins petitioned the government for control over their traditional lands and were turned away. In 1979, the Algonquins issued a joint resolution with other Algonquin communities (Maniwaki, Lac Simon, Grand Lac Victoria, and Abitibiwinni) calling for "the area situated within the boundaries of Parc la Verendrye [to] be henceforth reserved for hunting, fishing and trapping exclusively by the Algonquin people." Instead, the Québec government has actively promoted the park to attract sport-hunters and canoe tourists. Today, the province reaps millions of dollars annually from the permits issued for hunting, fishing, and camping within the park, while the Algonquins receive nothing from the activity taking place on their lands.

Blockade

By the 1980s, more than thirty-eight logging companies had leases in the ABL's territory. The provincial government had begun to issue twenty-five-year, non-revocable logging concessions to companies like Canadian Pacific Forestry Products (now Domtar), to clear-cut large areas of La Vérendrye Wildlife Reserve. New logging roads cut fresh pathways through the territory, along which timber was extracted and sport hunting flourished. Despite these incursions, the ABL continued to practice their traditional ways of life, but under tremendous threat – not only was the natural habitat being destroyed by logging, but pesticides and herbicides were sprayed, killing vegetation and poisoning animals.

The ABL had already begun a campaign of blockades to protect the forest when the UN Brundtland Report (1987) was released. The report suggested that indigenous people should play a significant role in managing the sustainable development of natural resources. Sections of the report were translated into Algonquin and discussed with elders and community members. The Barriere Lake Algonquins were attracted by the concept of sustainable development, which explicitly recognized the needs of future generations. The ABL, under Customary Chief Matchewan, demanded that the Canadian government act on the report's recommendations by allowing them to implement a conservation strategy on their territory, but the government continued to ignore their concerns.

The Algonquins took matters into their own hands, occupying Parliament Hill in 1989. They faced the Crown in federal court for this protest, ready to challenge their eviction from unceded Algonquin territory until the Crown got nervous and stayed the charges. When the ABL set up blockades to stop chemical spraying, Québec finally backed down. The community persisted and moved their protest camps to block six new logging roads. Their actions culminated in a blockade of provincial highway 117, a major regional artery for resource extraction.

Norman Matchewan, youth community spokesperson for the ABL and son of former Customary Chief Jean-Maurice Matchewan, was a child at the time of the blockades, but he remembers the conflict clearly:

> In 1989, I remember the blockades we had near La Domaine,
> a forty-minute drive down the road from Rapid Lake where

our community lives. These blockades lasted for a long time. I remember my Dad being attacked by the Québec Provincial Police. I was told about another fight my great *kokom* faced while out hunting. She killed a moose and the game warden tried to take her moose, but she didn't want to let it go. She put up a fight and was hit in the head with a rifle, leaving a big cut across her forehead. The violence my father later faced in the 1990s and I am facing today echoes what my great *kokom* went through to protect our rights. This is my community's struggle to protect our way of life and our land.

Occurring during a provincial election, the 1989 blockades began to attract politicians' attention: all it took was a visit from a PQ candidate for the Liberal provincial Minister of Indian Affairs to swoop down in his helicopter for a quick chat. John Ciacca replaced Raymond Savoie after the election and flew over in a helicopter from Oka the morning after the 1990 highway 117 blockade to discuss an agreement.

ABL's Trilateral Agreement

After two more years of blockades, negotiations, stalling, and debate over water bodies in the territory an agreement was finally arrived at in 1991. The Trilateral Agreement, between the ABL, Quebec, and Canada would give the Algonquins ultimate decision-making power over resource management on the land entrusted to them by their ancestors.

The United Nations hailed the agreement as "trailblazing" and the Royal Commission on Aboriginal Peoples (RCAP) suggested that it represented a strong model for moving forward with First-Nations-Canadian relations:

> Not infrequently, co-management regimes are embarked upon without the funds, database, collective political will and 'vision', that are such vital ingredients to make a regime work... In contrast, the Trilateral Agreement provides for the time, the funding and the organizational infrastructure to create a database, a plan and a 'mindset' among all participants, to make a future partnership in resource management work.

Technically, the Trilateral Agreement is a study and recommendation process agreement. Practically, it is an arrangement between the Canadian state and the ABL that gives

Barriere Lake a decisive voice in the management of 10,000 square kilometers of their traditional territory, protects Algonquin land uses, and gives them a share in the resource-revenue from natural resource development on their land.

This arrangement would still mean little if it did not provide the ABL with the financial resources to collect, correlate, and map the community's traditional knowledge of their land. Without detailed maps of traditional land use, having a "say" at the table over resource management would be reduced to hazarding guesses or doing lengthy consultations with elders for each individual proposal for logging or resource extraction.

The government agreed to fund these traditional land use studies. Thousands of hours of oral history and traditional knowledge were incorporated within sophisticated Geographic Information Systems (GIS) maps that include, for example, Algonquin place names, winter camps, and animal migration routes. This knowledge set the frameworks and recommended regulations for such conservation concerns as the distance tree-cutting can come to sacred areas, plant harvest sites, cemeteries, and spawning regions of the watershed. Furthermore, as opposed to most land claims agreements, the Trilateral Agreement "creates an interim management regime which freezes further deterioration of the resource base" (RCAP, 1995).

The collection, inventory, study and analysis of data about renewable resources and their uses is the first phase of the Trilateral Agreement, and the preparation of a draft Integrated Resource Management Plan (IRMP) is the second. Although the agreement set out completion of the process by 1995, because of delays in the agreed upon process caused first by Québec (1991-1993) and then by Canada (1996-1997), the 1995 target wasn't reached. In December 1996, Indian Affairs Minister Ron Irwin sent a letter affirming that the federal government would continue funding the Trilateral Agreement process. In fact, the federal government continued funding their portion of the 1991 Trilateral Agreement process only until July 2001 when then Indian Affairs Minister Robert Nault unilaterally withdrew from all ABL agreements. Québec funded the remaining Trilateral Agreement work, including part of Canada's portion, from 2002 until 2006-07.

Phase three of the Agreement – the formulation of recommendations regarding implementation – was to involve developing:

a draft ecosystem-based Integrated Resource Management Plan (IRMP) with a commitment to the principles of sustainable development, conservation, protection of the traditional way of life of the Algonquins, and versatile resource use, and to reconcile forestry operations and sports hunting and fishing with the environmental concerns and traditional way-of-life of the Algonquins of Barriere Lake.

Due to the pullout of the federal and provincial governments, the third phase process of the Trilateral Agreement Phase has not been completed and Canada's fiduciary obligations under this Agreement have never been fulfilled. The real threat posed by the Trilateral Agreement is the possibility that other indigenous nations might consider it as an alternative model to negotiating the use and ownership of their unceded territory under the Comprehensive Land Claims (CLC) process. As RCAP strongly underlines:

> It must be emphasized that the Barriere Lake Trilateral Agreement has many inherent characteristics that suggest its applicability under widely varying circumstances. Most importantly, it is a well thought-out and politically non-threatening approach to co-operative sustainable development.

The CLC process forces negotiating bands to extinguish their Aboriginal rights and title, convert their communal land into "fee simple" (private property), and mortgage the cost of maps and legal fees against any financial settlement they might receive. On the other hand, the Trilateral process ensured that the government would fund comprehensive land use studies while giving the community a decisive role in resource management both during and after negotiations – without putting their Aboriginal rights and title on the negotiating table.

Subsequent conduct has cast serious doubt on the sincerity of government promises to ever honour their word and implement the plan in full. Instead of signaling the end of a long and difficult fight to assert their rights, the signing of the Trilateral Agreement marked the beginning of an even more treacherous struggle for the Barriere Lake Algonquins.

Thirteen Years, Two Coup d'États

During the Trilateral Agreement's first phase, which provided research funding and interim measures to harmonize logging with

Algonquin land uses, Québec and Ottawa dragged their heels. The money needed to undertake the work was not forthcoming.

However, after resuming funding for the Interim Resource Management Plans (IRMPs) in 1996, the Department of Indian Affairs changed tactics. They rescinded recognition of the Customary Chief and Council and appointed a small faction within the community, many of whom lived outside the reserve and were keen on seizing a piece of the logging revenue, as an "Interim Band Council."

The ABL have never accepted the Indian Act's electoral band council system. Instead Hereditary Chiefs and Councilors are nominated by an Elder's Council and selected in community assemblies. The community assemblies are open only to Barriere Lake adults who speak the language, live on the traditional territories, and maintain a connection to the land. After the faction submitted a signed petition, Indian Affairs claimed the community's leadership customs had evolved into "selection by petition" and recognized the dissident faction as the legitimate government. To make matters even worse, the ABL were placed under Third Party Management, which mandates that an external consultant unilaterally run the community's finances.

The Indian Affairs-supported leadership was rejected by the community and forced to rule as a "government-in-exile" from Maniwaki, a town 130 kilometres to the south. The majority of the community blocked the roads and refused to let this council back onto the reserve. Through 1996, the dissident group received millions of dollars from Indian Affairs while the community in Barriere Lake was deprived of basic funding for employment, social assistance, electricity and schooling for over a year. "The whole community got together, and survived on the traditional territory," according to Elder and former band manager Michel Thusky. The Trilateral Agreement was suspended during this period and logging in the territory resumed. Despite the dire poverty of the isolated community, blockades were erected and maintained through two harsh winters in an attempt to stop the logging.

Word of the community's struggle began to get out to church groups, media outlets, and activists in the community. Michel Gratton, a former provincial cabinet minister, admonished the Federal government in a letter to the Montreal Gazette:

> This unilateral decision to replace the Chief and council... is the imposition and diktat of raw power by the department against a small community without the resources or ability to defend itself.

Mediation in 1997 finally resulted in the reinstatement of the Customary Chief and Council; Indian Affairs agreed to restore the withheld funding, move forward with the Trilateral Agreement, and build housing, and to help bring electrification to the community. To avoid any future conflict over their governance procedures, the community codified their traditional laws, Mitchikanibikok Anishnabe Onakinakewin, into a 'Customary Governance Code.' Superior Court Judge Paul concluded that their customs had not "evolved" into selection-by-petition, as the dissident faction and Indian Affairs had claimed, and judicial review later revealed that Indian Affairs had advised the small "guerilla" group to submit the petition. One year later, the provincial government signed a "Bilateral Agreement" and a "5 Year Global Proposal" with the community, committing to expanding the land base, to revenue sharing, and to the building of new houses, a school, and other community infrastructure.

In 2001, the federal government walked away from the negotiating table one month before the first phase of implementation of the Trilateral Agreement was to be completed. Québec agreed to keep funding the Trilateral IRMPs and in 2006, John Ciacca and Clifford Lincoln were named as special negotiators, submitting seven Joint Recommendations as mandated under the agreements, specifying (among other things) revenue sharing, reserve land expansion, hydro-grid electrification, and the establishment of a co-management committee to implement the plan. All of these recommendations have been ignored.

Community members today believe that Indian Affairs is back to its old tricks. In 2006, Jean Maurice Matchewan was re-elected Customary Chief, but a small faction ran a parallel leadership selection, claiming to have adhered to the Customary Governance Code. Indian Affairs refused to recognize Matchewan, and for a second time put the community under Third Party Management claiming it was justified by Barriere Lake's large deficit and uncertain leadership situation.

The Customary Elder's Council immediately challenged the decision in federal court, arguing that the deficit issues could be cleared up if the money owed to Barriere Lake from the 1996 funding deprivation was repaid as promised. But in the yearly funding budget, negotiated by the Third Party Manager and Indian Affairs in 2007, the money owed by the government was simply struck from the record. Another coup d'état had taken place, only this time the DIA refused to recognize any new chief.

Superior Court Judge Paul confirmed the legitimacy of Matchewan's council in yet another round of mediation in spring 2007, calling the government-sponsored challengers a "small minority" who "did not respect the Customary Governance Code." Matchewan's council was reinstated, but a year and a half later Matchewan stepped down as Chief. The Elder's Council and community selected Benjamin Nottaway as Acting Chief, but the dissidents agitated once again and in January 2008, they held their own elections and were recognized by the Department of Indian Affairs as the legitimate government. Even the court worker assigned to observe the process put in writing that he couldn't confirm the legitimacy of this council.

New Chief Casey Ratt insists he has the support of a majority of the community this time, but has refused to enter the leadership re-selection process demanded by the Elder's Council to settle the dispute.

Indian Affairs says it plans to take the new council off Third Party Management, something the previous leadership was never offered. The new council has indicated that it plans to quash the court case challenging the federal government for unfairly imposing Third Party Management and for breaching the Trilateral Agreement.

Meanwhile, Québec has sat for a year-and-a-half on the provincial Joint Recommendations for its Trilateral obligations. But even with Québec's agreement, the Trilateral Agreement could only go ahead with federal co-operation.

Marylynn Poucachiche, youth spokesperson for the community and coordinator of the volunteer school says:

> I think the government has us where they want us, fighting with each other and forgetting about the real issues.... they can then keep exploiting our land and renegotiate the outstanding issues on their terms.

The Situation Today

Since March 2008, the community has organized a number of marches in Ottawa, has occupied local MP Lawrence Cannon's office, and has traveled to Ottawa, Montréal, and Toronto giving public talks to raise awareness about their cause and the situation in the community. As a last resort, the community took the difficult decision to blockade provincial highway 117 on October 6, 2008.

Community spokesperson Norman Matchewan explains what happened:

> To avoid negotiations, the government allowed Monday's peaceful blockade to be dismantled by the Sûreté du Québec (SQ), which without provocation shot tear gas canisters into a crowd of youth and elders and used severe "pain compliance" to remove people clipped into lockbox barrels... We set up the blockades Monday morning as a last resort, to inspire in the government a changed attitude. Our good faith and patience and reasonable demands have so far been rewarded by broken promises, deceit, and deplorable interventions. Is this all we can expect? (See October 8 posting on www.barrierelakesolidarity.blogspot.com for Norman Matchewan's full op-ed in the Montreal Gazette).

There was worse to come. With no government response, the ABL erected blockades again on November 19. This time, the SQ targeted community spokespeople and leaders, arresting Acting Chief Benjamin Nottaway and Marylynn Poucachiche, among others. The Chief was jailed for forty-five days in Ottawa. Since March 2008, over forty people from the community have been arrested and charged.

One sign of hope are the federal court cases pursued by the Elders Council of the community against the Minister of Indian Affairs – one challenging the government's decision to put the community under Third Party Management, the other launching a judicial review into the conduct of the Minister for recognizing the Ratt council in violation of the Customary Code, which constitutes an abrogation of Aboriginal rights and title. In the latter case, a rare judicial review has been granted the Elders Council and the actions of the Minister will soon bear judicial scrutiny and, hopefully, be called to account.

In their language, Algonquin peoples call themselves Anishnabec, meaning "original people," or more generally "human being." As Pete di Gangi, Director of the Algonquin tribal council once wrote, in the face of all this, traditional Algonquin conservation strategies have survived:

> Despite years of sustained negative impacts, Algonquin use of fish and wildlife resources within their traditional territory has persisted. Perhaps even more important, Algonquin management techniques have continued to be applied wherever and whenever circumstances have permitted.

There is a saying in Algonquin among the elders, "Aki kina awek kedoja madizi" – "the land is for everyone." The Algonquins of Barriere Lake are defending their land not only for their own future generations, but for all future generations. The time has come to join them.

Solidarity

In February 2008, one month before the latest coup d'état, a group of Montréal activists traveled to the Rapid Lake reserve. At a community meeting, they presented a request to do solidarity work with the Algonquins and a relationship was formed. The Barriere Lake Solidarity Collective was created in Montréal soon after the visit, with solidarity groups following in Ottawa and Toronto. Leadership has been taken from ABL community members and, save for minor exceptions, supporters have not undertaken to speak on the community's behalf without permission.

I cannot speak on behalf of the solidarity collectives but I can give an impression of the work that we are doing. The Montréal, Toronto, and Ottawa solidarity groups work on joint initiatives, but are relatively autonomous. Montréal is the most active group with the largest membership, but each group makes strong contributions to the effort. The solidarity groups have hosted public speaking events with community members, undertaken extensive media and outreach campaigns, brought dozens of supporters to the first and second blockades in October and November 2008, organized fundraisers, and helped plan marches, actions, and other protests.

What I find most productive about the work of the solidarity committees has been the emphasis on creative campaigns and cultural production; on historical and political analysis of Canadian colonial policies; and on forming relationships with ABL community members. In particular, Montréal activists initiated "Mitchikinabiko'inik Nodaktcigen" ("Radio Barriere Lake") on the reserve and are helping with an alternative community economic development project of crafts marketing. "Barriere Lake Anishnabe Kachigwasin," a film produced by Martha Steigman about the first blockade, with footage later included of the second, rapidly became a viral video that has garnered national and international attention for the community.

Montréal activists also initiated a call-in campaign targeting Indian and Northern Affairs Canada (INAC) officials, spending many cumulative hours locked in a serious debate with bureaucrats about the Trilateral Agreement. The capacity for activists to call INAC and get into high-level debate about the fiduciary responsibilities of government, the details of the Trilateral, and the history of INAC's actions towards the community can perhaps be attributed to the fact that a central focus of the solidarity groups has been research and popular education on colonial history and policy in Canada. As a result we have been able to develop considerable fluency in the particular and complex legal, constitutional, and political history of dispossession in the particular case of the Algonquins of Barriere Lake.

Although much more space would be needed to adequately describe the challenges involved in doing this solidarity work, several issues are worth calling attention to. First, the complexity of the political narrative of Barriere Lake may have demanded a high level of engagement by activists, but this has also proved challenging for media, activists, and other groups to grasp. Secondly, the ABL dissidents have lashed out at the solidarity groups, even blaming them at times for contributing to the crisis. Thirdly, while the size of the community is small enough that there is little confusion about trustworthy gatekeepers and spokespeople, the challenge is precisely to not become a burden for the few spokespeople the community makes available, and also to remain mindful of uneven access to resources – money, phones, and internet access – which can make communication and organizing difficult. Nonetheless, as with any meaningful, responsible relationship, this one continues to be negotiated and redefined. Only time will tell what the long term effects of this work will be. In the meantime, word has gotten out about the situation at Barriere Lake, and that seems a victory in itself.

Urban supporters in today's solidarity groups are certainly not the first supporters of the ABL's cause and they will not be the last. During the late 1980s and early 1990s, ABL community spokespeople traveled to give talks in cities on a regular basis. According to Jean-Maurice Matchewan, the community's supporters have also included non-native Québécois supporters on the early blockades and allies among other nations and organizations he met at a United Nations assembly in Geneva, where Matchewan traveled in the late 1980s to present the ABL's case.

Native support has also been offered in many forms. First and foremost, the Algonquin nations that form the Algonquin Nation Secretariat tribal council along with Barriere Lake – Wolf Lake and Timmiskaming – were extremely supportive of the Trilateral

Agreement, signing a resolution early on allowing Jean-Maurice Matchewan to go ahead with it. Other Algonquin nations outside of the tribal council have been less supportive.

The youth who have taken up the mantle of struggle today are beginning to forge new relationships with indigenous communities across Turtle Island. In November 2008, three ABL members drove to Winnipeg for the "Defenders of the Land" conference, which brought together First Nations activists from across the country to share stories and strategize about developing unity and solidarity across nations. This opportunity to meet people from other First Nations communities led to a "Native Caravan," which involved two Barriere Lake community members traveling with supporters to Tyendinaga Mohawk Territory, Six Nations, and to Ardoch Algonquin Nation.

The intergenerational nature of the struggle is key to understanding how a community can continue to struggle without losing heart or losing sight of the goal at hand: the land. On this theme, and the themes of renewal, resistance, and struggle, I will leave the last word on Barriere Lake to Norman, Jean-Maurice Matchewan's son:

> [At first] I was young and unaware of the significance of what was going on; I was just observing. Now in my twenties, I understand what they were fighting for and I will continue to do the same. I grew up connected to the land. I did my harvest with my family and I know how important the land is to us – to Anishnabek people. Harvesting from the land is our means of survival. Our language survives through our continued connection to the land. ★

Notes

1   Acknowledgements and sources: An excerpt from an article on the recent history of Barriere Lake written by Montreal Barriere Lake Solidarity Collective member, Martin Lukacs ("Coup d'état in Indian Country," first published in the Dominion.org on April 18, 2008) appears blended into the story about the three coup d'états presented above. Other research, writing, and excerpts on Barriere Lake were contributed by Montréal Barriere Lake Solidarity Collective member Charles Mostoller. Thanks also to Russell Diabo, policy consultant to the Algonquins of Barriere Lake for over 20 years (and tireless explainer of the white man's cunning) for his contribution to this essay. Russell's recent public lectures on the struggle at Barriere Lake informed much of the historical account and political analysis of this work. Some of the main sources drawn upon for this work remain the intellectual property of the community and have never been published or publicly cited. These works include Peter Douglas Elias' epic work, "Socio-Economic Profile of the Algonquins of Barriere Lake," dated January 1996, then revised in August 2002; James Morrison's "Algonquin History of the Ottawa Watershed" prepared for Pete di Gangi, Director of the Algonquin Nation Secretariat, and dated November 26, 2005; and Pete di Gangi's discussion paper, "Algonquins of Barriere Lake: Man-Made Impacts on the Community, Fish & Wildlife, 1870-1979," dated March 2003. Material relating to the ABL in the 1995 Royal Commission on Aboriginal People (RCAP) can be found online at http://sdcanada.org/images/sb1/RoyalCommissiononAboriginalPeoples-BL-relevant-content-from-Ch4.pdf. Also of relevance is the article "A Perspective from a Barriere Lake Algonquin Youth: From Tikinagan (cradleboard) to Spokesperson," *Redwire Magazine*, Vol 11, Issue 2. All other information presented here is derived from primary resources, including audio recordings, presentations, government and tribal council documents which can be found at: www.barrierelakesolidarity. blogspot.com/2008/03/resources.html.

THE NORTHEASTERN ANARCHIST

CLASS STRUGGLE THEORY & PRACTICE

from **NEFAC**

Northeastern
Federation of
Anarchist
Communists

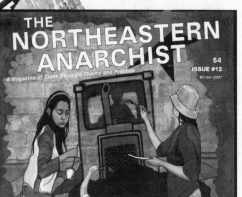

THE NORTHEASTERN ANARCHIST
$4
ISSUE #12
Winter 2007
A Magazine of Class Struggle Theory and Practice

Checks and money orders can be made out to "Northeastern Anarchist" and sent to:

The Northeastern Anarchist
PO Box 230685, Boston, MA 02123, USA
northeastern_anarchist@yahoo.com

Name:

Address:

City   State   Zip   country

email

Total **back issues** _____ ....x $2 _____

Entire set of back issues (#1-12) ......$22 _____

bundle orders for distribution _____
. . . x $3 per copy for five or more copies
. . . x $2.50 per copy for ten or more ...... _____

Subscription (4 issues) .... $15 _____

Solidarity Subscription.................$25 _____
support free subs for prisoners

International orders ......please add $4 _____

anonymous **contribution** ....$ _____

TOTAL: _____

NEFAC.NET

A Culture of Resistance

Lessons Learned from the Student
Liberation Action Movement

Suzy Subways

In March 1995, 20,000 students from City University of New York (CUNY) were attacked by police after surrounding city hall to protest a draconian tuition increase. This protest, organized by the CUNY Coalition Against the Cuts, marked an upsurge in student movement activity that continued into 1996, when the group transformed into the Student Liberation Action Movement (SLAM), a multiracial radical organization. Before disbanding in 2004, SLAM established chapters at CUNY colleges in all five boroughs of the city. This roundtable focuses on the chapter at Hunter College in Manhattan and explores SLAM's legacy of building a left culture in New York City and across the country.

SLAM's legacy is bound up with the evolution of CUNY, which became the primary route out of poverty for the city's Black, Latino, and immigrant communities starting in the 1970s. Prior to that, despite offering free education since 1847, CUNY was predominantly white. In 1969, Black and Latino students at City College in Harlem, with support from the Black Panthers and Young Lords, occupied CUNY campus buildings and won an open admissions policy that made CUNY accessible to students who needed remedial classes because they had attended substandard high schools. By 1976, the year CUNY started charging tuition, the student body was predominantly people of colour. The policy of open admissions was reversed in 1999, despite SLAM's militant opposition. This roundtable is part of a larger and ongoing SLAM oral history project (see http://SLAMherstory.wordpress.com). While many people helped build SLAM, this article highlights the voices of some of the women of colour members. These women represent different generations of SLAM, from founders to younger leaders. Their insights convey their experiences in SLAM and draw out lessons about building organic leadership and creating multiracial, feminist organizations that are accountable to communities directly affected by the issues.

Lenina Nadal was a founding member of the CUNY Coalition Against the Cuts and SLAM. Having graduated in 1997, she returned in 2000 to help create SLAM's organizer training institute. She is a filmmaker, playwright, and poet, and works for the Northwest Bronx Community and Clergy Coalition. Visit http://www.performingprofound.com

Rachèl Laforest was president of Hunter College's Black Student Union in 1995 and SLAM's first student government president in 1996. Before leaving SLAM in 2003, she defended open admissions and worked on SLAM's High School Organizing Program and the Mumia Youth Task Force. She is Director of Organizing for New York City's Transport Workers Union (TWU, Local 100).

Luz Schreiber worked on SLAM's open admissions campaign and other projects between 1998 and 2000. Co-founder of Ollin Imagination (a cultural circle of resistance of parents, artists, students, and educators of colour), Luz is a creative writing major and Hunter Student Union organizer.

Suzan Hammad was president of Hunter's Palestinian Club before joining SLAM and becoming a lead anti-war organizer in the early part of this decade. She is a painter (see www.cafepress.com/LailatiNar) and continues fighting for a free Palestine.

Tamieka Byer organized college and high school student walkouts against police brutality and the Iraq war as a member of SLAM between 2000 and 2004. She currently works with Amnesty International USA as the Board Liaison.

How did student clubs at Hunter come together in 1995, work in the CUNY Coalition, and start SLAM?

Suzan: Pre-SLAM, some of the first CUNY movement meetings were happening in the Palestinian Club. It was like we were all saying the same thing: "Oh shit, they're raising our tuition! Oh shit, they're bombing Palestine! Oh shit!"

Lenina: There was a lot of anxiety among the students, because tuition was going to be raised by $1,000. The Black Student Union had members who were responsible for some of the major takeovers of the Hunter campus and other CUNY campuses in 1990 and '91. The other clubs that had political consciousness included the Palestinian Club and the Arab Club, which were very strongly affiliated. And right across the hall was the Puerto Rican Club, which had some progressive membership. Those were the organizations that solidified people of colour on the Left.

The only alternative we were being offered was from the New York Public Interest Research Group (NYPIRG), which was like, "Let's lobby our representatives to see if we can change it from within." But the frustration was already building up and working class students were feeling like this might be the last chance they would have at a CUNY education. The stakes were very, very high. It was really a mass movement. It's like most movements – the leadership can claim it, but they have to claim it after the masses have already said, "This is what we want." Those of us who had been part of organizations, or who grew up with leftist parents, started to get to know each other and see that we had something to offer to sustain a movement. That's how some of SLAM's leadership started to come together.

SLAM was a student group. Why did it fight for political prisoners, visit Zapatista communities, bring medical supplies to Iraq, and protest police brutality and the navy occupation of Vieques?

Tamieka: CUNY doesn't exist in a vacuum. I mean, you talk about a tuition hike – which seems like a strictly CUNY issue – but you have to ask the question, "Why the hike?" The first thing I learned in SLAM was that tuition was free until the first year people of colour forced their way in. SLAM always made the point that tuition hikes were forcing out lower-income New Yorkers, while the government was spending more money recruiting these same lower-income people of colour to join the military.

Lenina: Despite the fact that SLAM had new leadership every year as people graduated and moved on with their lives, the last group of people in SLAM were still talking about police brutality and saying, "We can't forget what's going on in our own neighbourhoods." It was really amazing for me to see that a radical movement can be sustained if certain values are maintained. Instead of just a political organization, we developed our own culture to pass down.

Rachèl: There were a lot of young people on Hunter's campus who wound up being attracted to SLAM because we were speaking their language, politically and socially. Our Mumia Youth Task Force concert was a really dynamic event. We packed the entire 2,000-seat Hunter College auditorium. Mos Def and Dead Prez performed. People in the Mumia Coalition knew how valuable SLAM's level of organizing and sexiness was. Young people wanted to be around folks who really had their finger on the pulse of what was happening in terms of hip-hop. That's what made SLAM an easy thing to gravitate towards. Once you heard people talk about what they were really about, folks stuck around to listen and had ideas of their own.

I think the Amadou Diallo[1] issue made it easier to pull young people into the Mumia stuff. Even though young people had heard about Mumia, he wasn't a New Yorker. He wasn't someone that you might have seen when you left the house to go to school that morning. Amadou was. Especially for young people in the Bronx who lived right next to him, Amadou's murder and the acquittal of those cops allowed them to look at a situation like Mumia's, and really believe that he was framed for killing a cop.

There are serious lulls in organizing work, and sometimes events like this are catalysts. We realized that folks were angry because there were so many spontaneous gatherings throughout the city. Now, I have to tell you, I was very disappointed, because I think those mobilizations also showed how much people had gotten used to things. The response was angry, but I don't believe it went far enough. There were young people just running through the streets. But nothing really happened. When a community finds itself completely backed into a corner and is angry, fear drops away. Flipping over a police car, setting something on fire, rawly expressing the rage that you feel – there's nothing to hold it back. It showed SLAM that young people were so lulled by the system that they were angry, but they weren't angry enough. We weren't angry enough.

How did people bring in traditions of resistance from their own communities?

Lenina: People learned about who they were. A lot of people came out of the closet and started to engage in queer political theory by bringing that analysis into the organization to challenge people. We had a Cambodian member who was taken out of Cambodia during a very repressive time and brought to the US. She was discovering what the repression in Cambodia had to do with US foreign policy. Another member taught us how Mao used pop culture to create cultural resistance. He was saying, "how can we have our cultural resistance?" That's what helped feed Mao's revolution, and that was going to help feed our revolution. The Puerto Rican students and Black students had access to institutions created in the '60s and '70s by young revolutionaries like ourselves. Together, this created a very sensual space: it wasn't a clash of cultures so much as a joint discovery.

Rachèl: I was a red diaper baby. My parents were an interracial couple at a time when that wasn't popular in any way. My mom's parents had been union organizers; both were involved in the Communist Party during the 1920s and '30s. When I was younger, my mom was a tenant organizer. My father participated in one of the first formations of the Communist Party in Haiti. His family was asked to leave the country because of it. I learned that if there were liberation struggles that affected your life, you participated in them no matter what. SLAM was unique because most of the core group came from that kind of background.

Luz: The village in Oaxaca where I'm from has a great spirit of resistance, dating back to the Mexican revolution in 1910. I came to New York in 1998, four years into the Zapatista rebellion against neoliberalism's economic policies. People in Chiapas and elsewhere are displaced by these policies. The struggle in CUNY to keep admissions open was also about stopping students being displaced from the university. I was surprised that people in SLAM knew about the Zapatistas. From that, I knew that this was a group of people that cared about what was going on in the world and were eager to learn how indigenous people resisted. The Zapatistas declared, "We want a world that can fit many worlds," and that resonated with people everywhere. In New York there are many worlds, but the people in power don't want to make room for all of us.

How did SLAM develop leadership?

Luz: I think I was only able to imagine myself as a leader because I saw powerful Latina and Black women – leaders, intellectual, strong – doing stuff. They said, "We have to make you speak. There's a rally, and you have to testify because you're a remedial student." So they made me get up on top of a desk and recite a Nelson Mandela poem. It wasn't the most orthodox way to teach public speaking, but it worked. If someone had just said, "It's important to have women of colour leadership," that wouldn't have clicked as much as seeing it in practice.

Tamieka: Lots of trainings! Doing readings and coming back to the group to discuss them. And we were doing the readings while simultaneously doing the work: it was easy to look at something we had just read about imperialism and see how it was still relevant to how we interact with each other, and how America interacts with the rest of the world.

SLAM helped develop new leaders by actually having leaders that represented me. I've been at three other organizations since SLAM, and not once has there been more than one strong woman of colour at a time in each organization. In SLAM, part of what developed me was knowing that these strong women of colour had done the same readings I did, made many of the same mistakes I was currently making, and were the better for it.

Lenina: When we started the organizer training institute, we used the School of Unity and Liberation (SOUL) curriculum.[2] We recruited about 25 students a semester, and taught them organizing skills like campaign development, power analysis, public speaking, media relations and messaging, graphic design and web design. We also did political education using current events and older texts to define imperialism, patriarchy, and capitalism. In the high school organizing program, we had a video instructor. The young people were looking into the Anthony Baez[3] case, so they did a short documentary about that.

Suzan: I felt a very strong connection to our mentors from the Black Nationalist movement. They gave me good advice when I felt confused. I was mentored by their example of devoting their whole lives to the struggle for liberation and peace. They were experienced in organizing, and I really respected their anti-imperialism, anarchism, and Black Nationalism. Palestinians and the Black Panthers had worked together. To this day, not everyone works with Palestinians; we're still marginalized in the movement.

Why and how did SLAM become a women of colour-led organization? How did SLAM deal with questions of whiteness and male leadership?

Rachèl: The white men did much of the theorizing and writing. The women of colour did much of the relationship-building. The number of people recruited into the organization by white men was very slim. They built relationships with new people who didn't know them by having theoretical conversations about what was happening and pushed people little by little. The women – and mainly the women of colour – met people at a party or were handing out flyers and getting into a conversation about food or an event. They developed many more relationships at a time.

Internally, the women ran the show. Because we had a better understanding of the population we were dealing with and what folks were going to respond to, we made decisions about what should happen. While some of the white men in SLAM had some great ideas, sometimes people said no for the sake of saying no, just to not move on another idea the white man had put forward. People were angry about not hearing their voices come through in the work. It was in the second year that people started to shut them down, and it came out angrily at first, but eventually it came out respectfully and it was for the right reason. It wasn't to shush up the white man but because, "Actually, we genuinely don't think that's a good idea right here, right now. But we love you, and we want you to keep putting ideas out on the table."

Luz: I learned to become aware of power dynamics within the group. We called out white privilege, sexism, and homophobia during meetings or any kind of gathering. All these forms of oppression persist because we internalize them. At times it was challenging and even painful. But if a man spoke for too long, someone would ask, "So what do women think of this?" I wasn't used to seeing a man following a woman's direction or being challenged for his behavior, and that was amazing. Many men preferred to only engage in theoretical work, write articles, speak at meetings, and argue ideas. For a lot of men, it's easier to take on the role of the intellectual and leave the organizing and networking to women. The men in the group acknowledged that women were better at organizing. But sometimes it was a cop out: men aren't good relationship-builders because they don't practice or try hard enough.

Lenina: SLAM allowed people of colour to have their voices at the forefront by teaching people public speaking, writing, and documentation skills. For white people who have had some level of privilege, who are good writers or speakers, or who have had a good education, their role is really to be a trainer. And they can continue to write because if you're teaching someone how to be a writer, but you're also writing yourself, that person feels like, "I'm being taught by someone who really does this stuff and takes it seriously." You have to see if you can play a role in helping somebody who is afraid that what they say or how they'll say something won't be accepted. Historically it hasn't been.

How did Maoism and anarchism shape SLAM's decisions and goals?

Rachèl: Those ideologies were interwoven in the work. Anarchism shaped our involvement in the global justice convergence protests against the Republican National Convention in Philadelphia in 2000. What we learned from Maoism showed up in the more institutionalized organizing work we did in the High School Organizing Program, the Hunter clubs, and our community anti-police brutality work. All of the folks involved had a genuine desire to be led by those most affected by what was happening. Sometimes it was SLAM members, and sometimes it wasn't. And I think our struggle to be a multicultural, multi-ideological group allowed us to ask about the needs of a particular community and figure out what role SLAM could play.

The anarchists leaned toward Maoism because the majority of the group leaned toward a Maoist tendency. Folks that subscribed to more Maoist ideas felt safer playing on both ends and were excited by a lot of the anarchist ideas that were put on the table. However, the fact that we had this institution to run that was university-based and had rules and regulations played a role in quelling the more anarchist activities. The anarchist notion of tearing things down and resisting any structure that was not built by us was important. And where Maoism came into play was that it wasn't just tearing down for the sake of showing outrage. Institution building was meant to replace what we were tearing down with a different approach, new ideas, and a new way of relating to people. I think the two played hand in hand.

Luz: It was amazing to learn theory and see it applied. I remember a demonstration against Herman Badillo, a man on the Board of Trustees that wanted to end open admissions. This was someone who fought for education for minorities early in his political career, and then he made racist statements to the media about Mexicans. Coming from a Latino, it was internalized racism. He said things like, these short people from the hills are coming here and taking over our schools, and we can't allow this to happen. I was like, "fuck, this shit is real, this is not something from a book." We needed to challenge the ideology that people of colour were intellectually inferior, culturally inferior, and therefore had to be segregated and denied a right to education.

You can hear all you want about theory, the masses, and how class relations work, but it's experiences like this that really bring it home and make you understand not only intellectually, but with all your senses. Mobilizing people to fight police brutality and for Mumia Abu-Jamal put ideas into practice. It wasn't just preaching. Because then Mao only becomes a gospel; it's not something you can live. I lived it with SLAM. Not only "What does it mean that women were disempowered systematically throughout the centuries?" but also "What does it mean to have women leadership? How does that look, how does that feel?"

Lenina: SLAM's Little Red Study Group brought together a group of radical teachers and community organizers: people who wanted to have a more radical nonprofit space. We decided to study Marxism seriously. We studied a lot of Mao, a little queer theory, a little feminism. That group evolved into the New York Study Group, which includes former members of Standing Together to Organize a Revolutionary Movement (STORM).[4] We felt a kind of identification and connection with STORM because it had the same goals around women of colour-led organization.

How did SLAM's militance relate to issues affecting its members' communities?

Suzan: I really am glad we were very loud when the wars in Afghanistan and Iraq broke out in 2001 and 2003. I wish a lot of people had stayed that loud, maybe because I related to it so much, because I'm from the Middle East, and there's been a lot of war in my history. What happened in the Nakba 60 years ago is happening today in Afghanistan, it's happening today in Iraq. When we took over the Hunter president's office in February 2003, we just wanted to make a really bold statement. We met people that day who would later become SLAM members. Did we expect to stop the war that day? No. It was an expression of a lot of people's feelings of "Fuck this!" I think in America today, there's a lot of people suffering under the surface. I think people were feeling it, but nobody was saying anything.

Lenina: We believed we had to find the most revolutionary way to react. And that was being more militant at a time when this society was constantly encouraging us to be comfortable, passive, and do things without accomplishing anything. Militant action feels good because you're connecting and doing what's in your heart, despite whatever the state says. If you have a supportive community, why not take over a bridge? A lot of younger people tell us, "I wish I was around when SLAM was around." We used to say that about the Young Lords, and the Young Lords probably said that about somebody else. Just do the best you can, you know?

What were some of the contradictions in SLAM becoming student government at Hunter College?

Tamieka: Trying to appease the administration and still hold true to our politics at the same time. Making other student groups and clubs feel welcomed and not like SLAM was a special club that benefited from student government while they were given crumbs. Feeling overwhelmed with hard, emotional, full-time jobs at 20, 21, 22 years of age, in addition to SLAM work.

Lenina: I think you're hitting at the core of the nonprofit industrial complex. Any time anything becomes institutionalized, it loses a certain amount of energy. It's like running a small country like Cuba or Nicaragua, where you're no longer an outside guerrilla. All of a sudden we had money and power within the structure of our college. We had access to CUNY by-laws and knowledge of important meetings where real decisions were going to be made for students. We received this information in memos and we would raise hell in all those meetings. We had unlimited photocopying, and basically anything we needed for organizing (walkie-talkies, things we needed for rallies, for security), we could purchase with student government funds as long as we put it on the books. Plus, several organizations that weren't funded at the time – groups like Desis Rising Up and Moving (DRUM) and the Taxi Workers' Alliance –

could freely come in and use our copy machine, space, computers, and web access. Hunter was a hub for organizing work.

As time went by, we became a top priority for the Board of Trustees, which wanted to get rid of us. There were very explicit conversations about our organization. We took a very strong stance on Palestine in a city where, to be honest, it got us into a lot of trouble. And taking a stance on police brutality was very important to us, and we didn't give a shit. If it was going to mean losing student government, then F-it, you know?

Rachèl: We really did capitalize on a moment of a lot of young people being pissed off and wanting a space to channel that energy. You build institutions to try to carry people through the valleys until the next peak of movement activity arrives. People have to be better prepared, and have stronger and tighter language for how to talk about the peaks when they get there. But as far as our organizing capacity, I think it was a double-edged sword. SLAM could not have done the things we did without the resources student government provided. And I think the obligations to run the student government prevented SLAM from doing some of the greatest things it could have done. I lived in the office. I got caught up in so much of the financial bullshit that it didn't allow me to really go out amongst the students and talk about what SLAM did, why I was a part of it, and how important the issues we were dealing with were.

What do you think led to SLAM falling apart?

Rachèl: In 2000, it was easier to link police brutality to CUNY students. At that time, Hunter was still a majority of people of colour college, so students went home to the very communities we were talking about. Tuition was going up every year, so the class and complexion of the school changed. It became more of a challenge for SLAM to link the antiwar organizing with the student body because students didn't see the connection between undocumented immigrants being detained and CUNY students being targeted. They didn't see it as their struggle.

There was also a stigma tied to SLAM being in student government for eight years, as if it had been a dictatorship. Sometimes the student body didn't want to hear shit anymore.

Lenina: In the end, we were an institution getting money from students. A lot of the people who were getting a salary in SLAM didn't want to work on student issues. They wanted to work on issues in their communities. It wasn't too hard for the administration to tell the students, "These people aren't really serving you." The problem when you get money from any particular source is that you're beholden to that source of funding. Because open admissions ended, you began to see more middle-class students that were easily persuaded that we were a little too radical.

Also, when you have a job, it's no longer really a movement for you. It becomes your 9 to 5. You almost get sick of it, like any job. And it's funny, because small businesses are encouraged to constantly make people feel a sense of the team and a commitment to the cause. We didn't really do that, because we didn't know how. So we were functioning the way you would in a grassroots movement, where it's like, "You're not holding up your end of the stick here, what's wrong with you?" as opposed to "Let's go back to our mission, our values." What were we doing to heal ourselves, to reinvigorate ourselves, to keep ourselves excited and to be engaged and understand why this was so important? When you don't have that consistently, it's difficult. Especially when you have an administration connected to mayor Giuliani, and they're mobilizing against you, and you're doing your darnedest to stay in there, but you don't have as strong a connection to the student body that was initially so all about you being there.

Tamieka: The older generations of SLAM did the best they could with transferring information and skills to the incoming generation. Looking back, I see that there is a problem if the organization is unable to function without some of its founding members. If we can't survive without a member who has been in the organization for over eight years, then we're lacking the self-sustaining part, right? I look back and think, "Boy, if we had those contacts... I didn't know we had a contact in X organization! Wow, that could've been helpful." But folks get burnt out and are ready to wrap it up. We had a haphazard transfer of institutional knowledge. I've seen it everywhere; it's not just a SLAM problem. How to effectively pass knowledge and history along, and make sure new folks are receptive to this kind of learning. We all have such huge egos. I think too often we wanted to work on our own; we could've shouldered some of our work better if we partnered with more organizations, in my generation at least.

SLAM was great at movement building and leadership development, but not so successful at winning immediate victories. The loss of Open Admissions was especially painful. Why do you think SLAM lost so much, and how much do you think it matters?

Lenina: In 1995 they raised tuition by $750 instead of the initial threat of $1,000. Of course, the reformist groups took a lot of credit for that, like the threat of 20,000 young people showing up out of nowhere and running around Wall Street had nothing to do with it! The administration also didn't cut financial aid as much, but our vision was so much larger. We wanted a school where we didn't have to pay tuition, period. Some of the most amazing, transformative experiences are experiences where you lose. Those anti-globalization protests were so deeply transformative in terms of like, wow, we could actually build sectors of society with just who we have. We could build a little media sector and a little law sector, and a little sector of doctors, and we could really make this happen on our own. And we didn't win crap in that, you know?

Rachèl: SLAM chose issues sometimes that we knew weren't winnable, but were core issues that people could be unified and gathered around. And the strength built by people learning about each other and building that community was a kind of victory. If you are a longstanding organization, and you come down from a peak and you're in a valley for a while, there are times when choosing small, winnable issues is important for the morale of your members. People have to know that the organization has the strength to win things, even if they're tiny. But even if the issue itself is not winnable at this point in history it's a win to bring people together around it, especially if they're able to stay stuck together around that issue and grow outward. They say to pick your battles wisely, even in interpersonal relationships. And yeah, sometimes you only want to focus on the battles you know are significant to the relationship. And then other times, you just want to have the battle for the sake of making sure that something that's important to you doesn't just die by the wayside.

Suzan: Unfortunately, it's a very unfair power dynamic. The forces against us have a lot of power. But our spirit is stronger, and what we want is greater.

What can SLAM teach the CUNY movement and the Left today?

Rachèl: The one-on-one relationship-building approach to organizing. The internet makes it so that you don't have to be in human contact with anybody anymore, and that's not such a great thing. My first boyfriend at Hunter became politicized because every single time I saw him by the cafeteria, I would stop to have a discussion with him about what was happening in the Black Student Union, and how he might be able to get involved. You sort of met a friend and didn't let them go. Working at Jobs With Justice, they had me running around East Harlem, door-knocking, and they had this whole laid-out script that I never used. That Alinsky[5] style is devoid of any real, genuine investment in the issue. Because of SLAM, I had learned how to look for the elements in it that I identified with personally, and let that shape the discussion. And to sit down and try to figure out who folks were, where they were coming from, did this affect them, and if it didn't, why? Did it move them, and if it didn't, why? You've got to deal with people where they're at if you want them to move forward in another direction. I brought what I learned in SLAM about the relationship-building approach into my work at the transit union also.

Luz: One of the core philosophies in SLAM was the personal is political. We really took time to build relationships. Sometimes people think that part is not really organizing, because it's just social. But that's the foundation of organizing. If you cannot build personal relationships, how can you build organizational capacity? When people set up 1,000 barricades in Oaxaca in 2006 to protect themselves against the government, it was instinctual, because in Oaxaca people have really large, closely knit families. That is a natural social network. People were guarding all the entrances of town and if they said, "Go get your family," your family means like 200 people. In Oaxaca, those relationships are already built; you just have to tap into them. Here, you have to start from scratch.

For students who come to Hunter now, there's a student government in the service of the administration. Just knowing that there was this other alternative for so long is amazing. Some people can't get over it. They ask me, "How did it happen?"

I see less intergenerational work happening now. SLAM really had these mentors from older generations in the community; they weren't scholars. People who are active now at Hunter have a professor they look up to. Right now, everybody learns from each other, but I don't feel like there's leadership. Horizontalism is more attractive, because everyone gets to participate, and more ideas are exchanged. But I think it's equally important to have systematic accountability. Some people are very repulsed by the idea of leadership. But if there hadn't been true leadership in the Cuban revolution, it would have failed.

Lenina: We were visionary, because we weren't just about the economic revolution and the political revolution. It wasn't just about these capitalist pigs, and socialism was the answer; it was about how the hell does that relate to hip-hop? It's like, we're going to take this boring message, something you'd read in a newspaper, and present it in a way that you can understand, like something that happened to your mom or could happen to your best friend, and make it that personal and real for you. It was about love and kindness and getting excited, not just about a new, different type of social order. ★

Notes

1 Amadou Diallo was an unarmed 23-year-old immigrant from Guinea, Africa, who was killed on February 4, 1999, by four New York City Police Department plain-clothed officers. They fired a total of 41 rounds at Diallo, mistaking his wallet for a gun when he reached for his identification.

2 SOUL works to lay the groundwork for a powerful liberation movement by supporting the development of a new generation of young organizers, especially young women, young people of colour, queer youth, and working-class young people. See www.schoolofunityandliberation.org.

3 Anthony Baez was a Puerto Rican from the Bronx. He was killed in 1994 by asphyxiation during a chokehold by Officer Francis Livoti, after his family's football hit a police car.

4 STORM was a multi-racial, internationalist, left cadre organization based in the Bay Area from 1994 to 2001. See leftspot.com/blog/files/docs/STORMSummation.pdf.

5 Saul Alinsky wrote *Rules for Radicals* and has inspired many neighbourhood activist groups like ACORN that have single-issue campaigns. The Midwest Academy is a training center that draws heavily from Alinskyism.

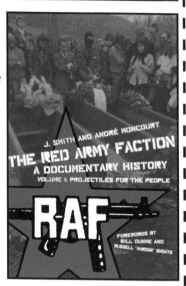

Navigating the Crisis

A Study Groups Roundtable

Dan Berger and Chris Dixon

Our moment is marked by both crisis and possibility. Economies are plunging worldwide, and ecosystems are in undeniable danger. State repression is expanding, and the US, Canada, and Israel continue to wage wars of occupation. In this context, the recent US presidential election tapped into a reservoir of popular energy for change. However, mass movements in North America continue to be relatively demobilized. The left itself is in crisis and lacks clearly defined visions and strategies. Although progressive sympathies now run high, progressive options – let alone radical ones – are few.

Radicals thus face urgent questions: How do we understand the current conditions and develop a revolutionary politics appropriate to them? How do we foster mass movements that can exceed "politics as usual" and burst into new fields of action? How do we create strategies that can activate popular sentiments? And how do we build organizations capable of advancing movements and consolidating gains?

One way that activists and organizers wrestle with these issues is through study groups – intentional spaces for critical and collective reflection. Study groups are a hallmark of the left. Previous periods of crisis, like the 1930s and 1970s, compelled radicals to jointly investigate theoretical and practical models of revolutionary struggle. Often, these investigations led to new organizations or campaigns. Similarly, the current crises have generated several formations that intentionally use study to advance political priorities and explore organizational forms. The following roundtable brings together four such groups in the United States:

Another Politics is Possible (APP) is a group of organizers and activists in New York City. Their core values include collective leadership, democratic self-determination, challenging all systems of oppression, and centering the experiences of people most targeted by these intersecting systems.

The Activist Study Circles (ASC) is a multi-tendency socialist study group in the Bay Area. It brings together Marxists, anarchists, and revolutionary nationalists committed to a racial, economic, social, and gender justice anti-imperialist politics and to building power in oppressed and working class communities.

LA Crew (LAC) is a collective that was brought together by a shared commitment to learn lessons from all of the rich traditions of liberatory resistance, and to engage others with their analysis and principles. The LAC studies, analyzes, experiments, and creates community through collectively agreed upon political work and shared principles.

The New York Study Group (NYSG) is a network of activists and organizers, mostly people of color, based in diverse communities and organizations in New York City. Since 2005, NYSG has been studying left organizational forms – mainly revolutionary parties and united fronts – and strategy.

These groups represent different, if overlapping, political strands. The tensions between their approaches, in turn, point to key unresolved questions concerning leadership, organization, and politics. Regarding leadership: Are leaders elected, established, or developed? Is leadership about exercising authority, manifesting group decisions, or developing collective power? Regarding organization: Should we be oriented toward a revolutionary party or set of parties, or should we discard the party model altogether? Can the party model co-exist with other models of revolutionary organization? Is a revolutionary organization committed to seizing power, redefining it, or something else entirely? And regarding politics: Are there important issues that we neglect by attempting to bridge multiple left tendencies, or do our political differences obscure common ground? These questions are not resolved here. Responses to these questions, meanwhile, expose differences not just of definition but of emphasis. Each group believes in building revolutionary organization(s), developing inter-left unity, and popularizing radical politics, yet they prioritize them differently.

The groups participating in this roundtable attempt to engage the perennial question – what is to be done? – by drawing upon an eclectic set of politics. The commitment to such politics varies: the NYSG draws explicitly from Marxist-Leninist history, APP looks to anti-authoritarian social movements like the Zapatistas, and the ASC and the LAC each work in their own way to bridge the divide. Despite these differences, all four draw from a range of tendencies on the revolutionary left, recognizing that whatever we build must both learn from and be different than what has come before. They suggest that, in responding to today's conditions, we must try to avoid the mistakes that revolutionaries of all stripes – Marxist and anarchist, revolutionary nationalist and identity-based – made in the past.

At their best, these study groups offer lodestars – orienting concepts rooted in practices – that we can use as we grapple with the pressing questions of our time. This roundtable thus sets a foundation for the kind of non-sectarian and principled debate we so urgently need. ★

Tell us about the origins of your study group.

APP: Another Politics is Possible first came together at the end of 2006 as a New York City-based study group of 15 organizers, activists, educators, dreamers, and revolutionaries committed to a collective process of self-education and political articulation.

We came together because of a shared practice. Many of us were already working in organizing projects and collectives to implement some aspects of the core principles that brought us together as APP. We were doing work on gendered violence, education, queer and youth organizing, childcare and community building primarily as members of immigrant and women of color organizations.

One of our primary intentions was to articulate a practice – a way of doing politics – that values collective leadership, seeks democratic self-determination for all people, and centers the experiences of people most targeted by the intersecting systems of patriarchy, capitalism, and white supremacy and their multiple permutations.

Building on this commitment, we align ourselves with those who argue that engaging state power is not enough. Drawing from the lived experience of decolonized states and from women of color feminist critique, we've seen that it's not just a question of *who* holds power but also *what form* that power takes. We've learned from history that when seizing state power is the primary strategy, it often ends by confirming Audre Lorde's sage wisdom that "the master's tools will never dismantle the master's house." We must work to reclaim, reimagine, and rebuild *our own* home. Creating liberatory forms of social organization beyond the state is a necessity. Attempts to model the society we envision transform our cultures and relationships, and create a guide for our politics and organizing. This prefigurative sensibility, popular in many of today's movements, has deep historical roots worldwide. These include forms of resistance that are often overlooked by traditional left analysis and range from communities of care to the transformative role of culture and spirituality in larger scale organized movements.

Some of the political questions we believe are fundamental to exploring different possibilities for revolutionary organization are: How do we both transform our interpersonal relationships and build broader cultures of liberation? What does collective leadership and democratic self-determination look like? How do we make sense of the many strategies to engage with the state as we seek liberation? How do we understand the process and significance of rebuilding community? How do we really build a movement that addresses the intersectionality of oppressions?

ASC: In the late 1990s, many longtime Bay Area organizing efforts were coming to fruition. They brought a broad range of people together around radical left politics and practice. September 11 changed the context of our struggle. Over the next few years, many of us brought our organizations and communities into the streets as part of the anti-war movement. During that period, leaders from different parts of the Bay Area left began conversations on building a broader socialist unity drawing from multiple traditions. This included communists developing new approaches to democratic organizing, grassroots power, and strategy, and anarchists developing new approaches to leadership, revolutionary politics, and anti-authoritarian organizing.[1]

In late 2003, a group of 30 of us from 20 organizations came together to think about what the Bay Area movement lacked and what we thought was needed. Out of that discussion a committee formed to plan a project called Movement Generation that brought together leaders in community-based organizations from different political traditions (Marxist, revolutionary nationalist, feminist, and anarchist) to engage in a nine-month study to develop strategy and guide our struggles. Through this process evolved a multi-trend movement building approach.

From this experience, a group of us decided in 2005 that we needed a study group to foster relationships and political unity in order to build left organization. Our planning committee met for about two years. We developed trust between us and trust in our ability to play a meaningful role in building a dynamic left. We then invited more than 100 people to participate and 80 of these went on to form the ASC program. We meet once a month in large groups, and then once a month in smaller groups to delve deeper into subject matter. We have continued as a group of about 40.

The study group began as, and continues to be, majority people of color, majority women, and a large percentage queer. To help create an intergenerational movement, we invited some older-generation comrades to participate. Most of us are in our late twenties to early 40s, with the majority in our 30s. We are multi-trend socialists (anarchists, Marxists, feminists, revolutionary nationalists, etc.) with demonstrated unity on key issues like anti-racism/anti-imperialism, the need for grassroots peoples' organizations to build powerful democratic movements, the need for a synthesis of left politics, and a desire to develop new politics and forms of organization.

LAC: Those of us who first began studying together had come to the conclusion that no single political trend had found the answer to creating the change we are fighting for. We concluded that every trend had lessons for us, both in their victories and in their failures. We came together to look at these trends and to determine what principles and strategies felt useful for leftists today.

The question of leadership has been central to our growth. Drawing from anarchist and horizontalist models, we hold each other accountable to the principle of non-hierarchy by "throwing power back." When we "throw power back," we commit to being "leaders" that inspire others to see themselves as agents capable of making social change, and to see their most important role as developing others to participate in making that change. We believe that everyone has the ability to learn from history and to participate in creating collective visions for the future.

Like Ella Baker said, "strong people don't need strong leaders." We see our group as a location to build strong people so they can in turn develop others to do the same. People have different levels of experience when it comes to reading, engaging with political ideas, and organizing. Because we want to create a space that's not dominated by the most "experienced" people, we aim for an equitable distribution and rotation of tasks and responsibilities. We encourage each other to take on roles that challenge us to grow in areas where we don't have much experience, and have a buddy system for supporting each other's development outside of meetings. We consciously challenge all the societal messages that tell us that "someone else is the leader."

NYSG: After a March 2006 discussion at the Brecht Forum on the need for a left party, five young activists and organizers from New York City came together to initiate a study group around the question of left organization. That first year of study brought together about 20 or 30 folks from diverse sectors of the social justice movement. Most of us were people of color in our 30s, politically active for more than a decade in a range of community-based organizations, and not ideologically fixed – some influenced by Marxism, some by anarchism, many agnostic or still figuring it out.

We started by studying the theories of the "united front" and the "revolutionary party," and by looking at the history of struggles in South Africa and the United States, and at new organizational models in Mexico and Brazil. During this first round, we found that we had some significant differences about the "revolutionary party" model. These tended to arise between autonomists, who wanted to discuss alternative organizational forms, and people from a range of ideological positions (Marxist, revolutionary nationalist, and "agnostic") who believed that revolutionary parties were necessary.

The participants who were compelled by the idea of a revolutionary party decided to initiate a second round of study. About 30 people came together to explore different historical models of revolutionary parties, learn from their contributions, and engage with their historical errors without abandoning them. This round of study was guided by two questions. First, what is our vision for a left organization/party that will help build a successful liberation movement in the United States? Second, how do we most effectively advance movement-building and left-building: by joining an existing left organization, initiating a new one, or something else?

At the end of this round of study, no individual from our study group chose to join an existing socialist organization, and no one argued for starting a new party. However, we all agreed that it was important to continue working with existing left organizations and invest in transitional projects that would lay a stronger groundwork for the re-emergence of a more relevant left organization in New York City.

In framing the objectives of our study, we skipped over a crucial step. We found that we couldn't figure out what kind of left organization we needed or how we might build one without a clear assessment of our political conditions and a strategic vision for the development of a successful revolutionary movement. We realized that we needed to re-open our study process and engage questions of strategy. That is the focus of our studies and dialogues over the next year.

What texts and movements have been instrumental to your study group?

APP: When we came together, we sought to locate our group in a historical and theoretical trajectory. Given what was happening in the world, we also sought to articulate what form our politics would take at a mass level.

Some of the texts we've read have focused on movements like the Adivasi of India, the Unemployed Workers Movement in Argentina, the Movimento Sem Terra in Brazil, the Zapatistas in Mexico, and the Black Freedom Movement in the United States. The critique of the not-for-profit industrial complex promoted by INCITE! Women of Color Against Violence provided an important lens through which to think about the weakened state of social justice movements in the US.

We have prioritized politics that are prefigurative, horizontal, autonomous, and based on the development of new social relations. Each of the movements we studied has also addressed the non-material dimensions of oppression, which include the ways it impacts our individual and collective emotional lives and the damage we inflict on each other and on ourselves. Frantz Fanon, Paulo Freire, and Audre Lorde have reflected extensively upon the ways that the oppressor's tactics permeate our interpersonal relationships and psyches. They have thus served as important examples of the need to integrate healing and self-care within a collective framework into our broader movement work.

ASC: Initially, the planning committee studied Martha Harnecker's essay "Forging a Union of the Party Left and the Social Left." Harnecker convincingly describes the need for anti-capitalists from the Party Left and social movements to come together and develop a new socialist politics together. For us, the Party Left includes traditional Left Party organizations as well as cadre organizations of various political stripes, like the Love and Rage Revolutionary Anarchist Federation, Standing Together to Organize a Revolutionary Movement (STORM), and the Malcolm X Grassroots Movement. Most of us come from the grassroots organizations, campaigns, and struggles of the social movement left.

We developed our study by voting on various case studies and themes. As a multi-trend group, it was important to us to select a set of case studies and readings that would help us to learn what we could take from each tradition. We began with an examination of the current moment. Studying the state of US imperialism, we took stock of our role as first-world leftists and discussed our visions of socialist politics for this century. From that grounding, we began looking at case studies of revolutionary organizations in various historic periods. We studied Guinea-Bissuea's national liberation struggle, which was very important to revolutionaries of previous generations but not so well known to radicals of our generation. We studied the Zapatistas' historical development and their contributions to current movements. This launched a larger discussion about Zapatismo and its applicability to the US. We explored the complex organizing strategies of the Communist Party in the US South during the Great Depression and the roles of the left in united fronts.

Our final case study focused on STORM in the Bay Area and the national Love and Rage Revolutionary Anarchist Federation. This allowed us to look at organizations from the 1990s in which some of us had been involved and brought us to a rich discussion on the role of contemporary third-world Marxist and anti-authoritarian/ anarchist organizations. Through all of these studies, we've tried to highlight both the successes and shortcomings of social movements in order to draw lessons for today.

LAC: We want to understand the diverse history of revolutionary movements – not just to develop our own theoretical foundation but to understand what other folks are drawing from and to develop our own critiques of different political trends. As the history of the 20th century shows, we don't think that any one trend "got it right." Nevertheless, many have something to contribute to a revolutionary politics for the 21st century. In our study, we try to grapple with the tension between useful insights, and limitations, obstacles, and contradictions. Within that framework, we study texts from the classical marxist tradition (Marx, Engels, Lenin, Luxemburg, Trotsky, Gramsci, etc.), third world marxism and revolutionary nationalism, Maoism, and the New Communist Movement, anarchist and autonomista movements, US people of color liberation movements, feminist and queer liberation movements, the Earth liberation movement, and others.

We also try to look at everything through the lens of what we call "unbreakapartability." Because oppressions are intersectional and affect all of us in complex and overlapping ways, the many forms of struggle for human liberation cannot be broken apart. An unbreakapartable approach aims to reveal that, as whole people, our struggles must reflect our whole selves. As well, unbreakapartability calls on us to learn from the vision and organizational forms of multiple struggles so we can build a truly integrated liberation movement.

NYSG: We studied the "classics" of Marxist thinking on the revolutionary party and united front (*Lenin's What is to be Done?*, Gramsci's political writings, and Mao's speeches on the United Front), looking to draw out the often-ignored dynamism and democratic thinking underlying these texts. We felt that Lenin and Gramsci demonstrated the important role of parties, the need to root those parties in popular struggles, and the possibility for a deeply democratic orientation.

Among the contemporary analytical pieces that we read, Harnecker's "Forging a Union of the Party Left and the Social Left" stands out. Harnecker distinguishes between the "party left," who are organized into explicitly socialist left organizations and parties, and the "social left" (which we have re-termed the "social movement left"), who are rooted in mass movements rather than socialist parties or organizations. She points out that both "lefts" have their own assets and challenges. She argues that we will only be able to build an effective left rooted in powerful social movements if we forge a "union" of these two "lefts." This approach helped us to identify the central role of building vibrant social movements that can help to reinvigorate the "party left" in the United States.

In our studies, reading history was just as important as theory. We found the history of the US Communist Party in the 1930s to be particularly helpful. The mass scale and revolutionary orientation of the CPUSA during that period inspired us to think bigger. We saw that revolutionaries need to be deeply rooted in mass struggle and guided by a clear strategy. We learned that revolutionary parties played an instrumental role in almost every serious revolutionary movement over the past century and that many of those parties made serious anti-democratic errors. We saw that revolutionaries needed to be deeply rooted in working class communities of color but that we also needed to build functional unity with broader social forces in order to contend for real power. Finally, we learned that cross-class and multi-racial alliances encounter serious pitfalls.

Has your group worked together politically beyond study? How has your study process affected your political practice?

APP: In the summer of 2007, we organized a delegation called "Another Politics is Possible: Living the Vision from Below and to the Left" to travel from NYC to Atlanta to attend the first US Social Forum (USSF). This delegation was the first time we worked together on a larger scale. We sought to embody the politics we had been articulating together through the journey itself. Instead of choosing a few individuals to travel by plane and renting hotel rooms for them alone, we raised funds for so that more than 70 women of color, mothers, children, youth, and childcare volunteers could attend the USSF. Ground transportation enabled more participants to attend, particularly immigrants and families with children.

We also used the USSF to collaborate with groups from around the country that had been exploring similar politics. Together, we created a 25-session track of workshops addressing topics like collective and non-hierarchical approaches to organizing, addressing violence against women of color through transformative justice, alternatives to institutional schooling, solidarity work, and community-generated visions and practices of autonomy. Several of the people we worked with on this track were beginning to form or were already participating in local study groups. Since the USSF, APP has teamed up with these study groups to engage in continued collaboration and dialogue.

ASC: Although we have moved away from the goal of forming an organization, we remain focused on building relationships and shared understandings to build the left. We put organization building on the back burner because of the need to bring together a large group of people engaged in many different areas of work. While we have unity on the political principles of the group, the level of experience working together varies widely.

We want to create space for discussions about larger questions of strategy and left organization. For example, many of us believe in the need to both build new forms of liberatory power and win existing power. However, what that means for organizational strategy is a question we want to explore. We are looking at various organizational forms because we believe there is much to be learned from both the Zapatista fight against neo-liberalism and the Communist Party campaigns during the Great Depression.

The ASC is not currently designed to take collective action. However, as individuals involved in other struggles, we have come together though long-term alliances, new campaigns, electoral work, fundraisers and cultural events, and new friendships. We hope the ASC will continue to foster a healthy left culture and allow us to find creative and meaningful ways to share common vision, analysis, and strategy so that we can move more effectively together.

LAC: After studying together for a few years, we formed a new collective, instead of joining an existing one. This was because we didn't see an organization that was drawing on multiple movements and deeply incorporating lessons from different trends. Our priority is building grassroots movements that can give masses of people the skills and vision required to transform the world. It is critical for us to find others who are committed to long-term movement building so that we can deepen our consciousness together. We believe in doing this within collective organization, where we can practice accountability and cross-sector coordination. Ultimately, this coordination should happen nationally and internationally as we have begun to see with the emergence of collectives that demonstrate how "another politics is possible" in the 21st century.

Within the LA Crew, we organize in education, healthcare, immigration, and the garment industry. We discuss our individual work collectively and look for opportunities to work across sectors. We are guided by six core principles: unbreakapartability, non-hierarchy, self-determination, experimentation, acknowledgement of our whole humanity – what we call "mind/body/spirit" – and dual power. This last concept flows from the history of popular movements creating alternative institutions that pose a revolutionary challenge to the system and lay the groundwork for a new society.

Our commitment to these principles shapes what we study and what we study shapes our practice. Our interest in dual power led us to study the Zapatista movement, which sparked questions about state power and the limits and benefits of dual power institutions. This impacted our thinking on the healthcare sector. Is it better to create small, model institutions or make demands on the state to provide universal access? How do we encourage people to think about the healthcare system they want while also taking advantage of opportunities to make system-wide changes?

NYSG: At the end of our second round of study, we were invited to help plan the Revolutionary Work in Our Times Summer School. Co-sponsored by Solidarity, Freedom Road Socialist Organization, the League of Revolutionaries for a New America, the LA Crew, and the NYSG, this four-day gathering brought together almost 200 revolutionaries and radicals from across the US (along with small delegations from Puerto Rico and Canada) in August 2008.

Helping plan the summer school reflected our conclusion that we need to overcome the history of sectarianism on the left and build unity among those committed to radical transformation of society. Based on the assessment that the "social movement left" has an important role to play in building a stronger left, we worked hard to recruit our comrades from social movement organizations to be participants and presenters. We hope the relationships people built through the school will provide a groundwork for developing the broad-based, movement-rooted, and ideologically diverse left organization we need today.

How has your group changed based on the challenges you've encountered while studying together?

APP: The successes, challenges, and limitations of our delegation to the USSF have greatly informed our second cycle of study and the ways we organize ourselves today. The experience of large-scale participatory democracy allowed us to engage our principles in practice. Our commitment to praxis left us with a series of new questions. Central themes that emerged included coordination, leadership, structure, organization, and transformative community building.

At the level of coordination, we've found it necessary to clarify that non-hierarchical-organizing doesn't mean a free-for-all or a disavowal of power dynamics. On the contrary, horizontal organizing requires intentional structure and coordination to directly address the different experiences and knowledge that people bring with them. While many of us have addressed these issues in our own collectives, we realized the need to develop a tighter and more transparent structure for APP.

Coming together for our initial round of study, many of us shared critiques concerning the patriarchal nature of the "charismatic" and individualized styles of leadership that have dominated many traditional forms of left organizing. As we grew, the need for a pro-active definition of leadership became increasingly clear. One of our current goals is to articulate an alternative leadership that emphasizes deep listening, actively nurturing a culture of participation in which everyone feels that their voice is valuable, and being cognizant of how power dynamics impact participation and emotional well-being.

ASC: It's difficult to create a space where our different socialisms can grow like flowers instead of like weeds choking the life out of each other. However, through the years of practice in our various organizations, through Movement Generation, and now through the ASC, we are developing left culture and practice that draws from our different strengths. As the ASC, we changed our goals on organization building as many of us had little experience collaborating with one another. We quickly learned that there was much to be done in terms of building our theoretical foundation and our capacity for political study. Despite these challenges, our primary goals of relationship building and bringing together larger segments of the left continued.

We struggle to simultaneously comprehend what we are studying and to draw meaningful lessons. While trying to see shortcomings in past experiences, it's important that we understand the conditions that impacted the decisions made in order to avoid sloppy and simplistic conclusions. We need to develop methods to understand our own conditions and possibilities. We need to remain humble and grounded when learning from the past and assessing political work today.

At times, people have critiqued the material we've read as being from one tradition or another. This has led the planning committee to ongoing solicitation of input from the membership. We've also struggled to maintain momentum and participation. In particular, while the ASC remained majority people of color, most of the people dropping off were people of color. Many have said that it was due to time pressures with their other work. We were also told that more follow up and reminder calls would help. The challenge remains creating participatory democratic processes when so many have so little time to participate. The planning committee of five recently expanded to eleven. We did this to build more leadership and increase participation, as we work to find a good balance between the planning committee moving the group forward and the larger group providing direction and focus.

How we work together is a critical part of the learning process. It's where we can experiment with the kinds of leadership and organization we need.

LAC: One challenge we've faced is getting people to feel comfortable reading and understanding difficult, primary source material – reading Lenin as opposed to reading a book about Lenin. People are sometimes challenged by the language and the references to people, groups, and events they don't know about. We also face the challenge of making such study accessible to non-

English speakers, people with children, and people not accustomed to study and reading as a form of learning.

We've tried addressing these challenges by reading "easier," newer things first, by creating activities that encourage drawing as a way of exploring ideas, and by using visuals for the material we cover. We also check in with people one-on-one as they are reading, before the group actually meets, to offer support and an opportunity to ask questions. Within the study group sessions, we use smaller break out groups to give people a chance to ask questions and "warm up" before large group discussion.

We've also found it important to incorporate our principle of mind/body/spirit into the study group process. This has meant giving people an opportunity to hear each other's stories, and creating a space where feelings have as much value as intellect. This seems to allow people to feel more comfortable. They take more risks in the statements they make and the questions they ask.

NYSG: We've struggled with the fact that our participants come with very different degrees of theoretical and historical knowledge. This is somewhat, though not absolutely, related to differences in educational background and pre-existing familiarity with explicitly left theory. It was difficult to find methods that would ensure that people were clear on the fundamentals and also challenge everyone to go deeper. We've worked hard to make our group accessible by combining training on fundamentals with critical engagement using both popular education and presentation-discussion formats. We've also invited people from different socialist organizations to help us unpack certain histories and theories. We've encouraged all participants to help plan at least one session, and have shared childcare costs.

Our study group has struggled with the tension between our ambition to build a stronger left and the fact that the many demands we face keep our level of capacity low. We also struggle to ensure that our study remains connected with the organizing work of our members. To deal with these tensions, we are currently working to develop a new structure that will alternate between smaller study groups (or "grupitos") based in our members' mass work and large group studies.

In light of the deepening economic crisis and the election of Barack Obama, how is your study group thinking about

the organizational and strategic demands of the current moment?

APP: In other regions of the world, we are able to identify truly transformative movements coordinated across issues, sectors, and communities. In Latin America, we take inspiration from the Zapatista-initiated Other Campaign, the powerful movements transforming Bolivia with and beyond the Morales government, and the Landless Workers' Movement of Brazil as it moves toward creating alliances with urban movements in response to the neoliberal policies of the Lula administration.

As of yet, there is no radical movement with such broad and deep roots here in the US that is either positing or building viable alternatives in the face of a worsening world-economic crisis. This is what we want to create. Today, there are more possibilities for democracy, justice, economic equality, and ecological sustainability than ever before. The deepening economic crisis has led to a generalized understanding that we need a new system. The Obama administration's response to some early mobilizations against the crisis suggests that more concessions can be won. The risk of cooptation, on the other hand, is much higher now than it was under the previous administration. The problems we face are global, however, and it is at this scale that we must ultimately be able to coordinate ourselves, both to fight back and to create new social relations.

ASC: We need a new kind of politics. This involves learning from the past but also looking at the moment in which we live. Socialisms of various sorts are in power again in Latin America. Anarchism and horizontalism are alive and well from occupied factories in Argentina to collectivized workplaces to Zapatista struggles. It's important to take direction from many quarters – from Freedom Road Socialist Organization, to community-based organizing in the Right to the City Alliance, to the Zapatistas – and try to draw together important lessons and insights that are relevant to our struggles.

Through our experience, we've come to face the question of how can we build a left that deserves to lead – a left that provides space for people to grow, study, heal, and get trained to build healthy self-governing communities that can transform society. This is happening throughout the country in thousands of organizations and projects. However, there is a tremendous need to create formal spaces to push to the next level. Many of us lack tools to make sense of the world around us. Many of us lack historical knowledge of our movements. We are struggling to move beyond comfortable left positions and place our revolutionary goals in the conditions we face. Our goal is not to be a marginal radical pole but to radically transform society.

As we begin our second round of study, we are focusing on national politics and strategy in this period of economic crisis and an Obama presidency. We are focusing on struggles for health care, immigrant rights, ecological sustainability, peace, and economic justice with the following questions: What is our vision and what are our transitional demands toward socialism? What should we be fighting for in this period? And what should left strategy be to both win immediate demands and build the power of working class and oppressed peoples? We are excited to step up to the challenges and opportunities before us, and the ASC is one space to help us do that.

LAC: We need to be flexible and encourage organizing and experimentation in many different spaces. The work we do today is like planting chamise, a brush plant native to California. When exposed to open flame, the chamise releases combustible gasses that accelerate the spread of wildfires. We can't predict exactly when and where these fires will start, but history shows us that people do rise up. Whether these uprisings can become movements powerful enough to transform society has a lot to do with the ideas that have been put out there and the organizing that has been done ahead of time.

The widespread energy created by Obama's election has ignited hope and inspired many people to believe in the possibility for change. We see this as an opportunity to encourage folks to engage in collective action to achieve broader changes instead of waiting for it to come from "above." The radical left's weak response to the economic crisis also teaches us that we need to break with old paradigms and experiment with new strategies for change.

Although we don't think it's particularly useful at this stage to develop a rigid view of which communities or sectors will be "in the lead" of future movements, our principles do guide how we prioritize where to work. Specifically, we try to make connections between different struggles. In our education organizing, we push for a vision in which the experiences and demands of teachers, students, and parents are seen as unbreakapartable. As we prepare for this year's May 1st actions, we are emphasizing cross-sector demands that point toward a broad popular response to the economic crisis. This means moving beyond a narrow focus on immigrant rights to include demands for housing, healthcare, education, access to food, and dismantling the security state.

NYSG: We find hope in several developments on the social movement left. In the last couple of years, social movements have consolidated into national formations such as Grassroots Global Justice, the Right to the City Alliance, and the National Domestic Workers' Alliance, and – in a different vein – the US Social Forum. But while the social movement left is the site of some of the most dynamic struggles, it remains limited by its relatively small scale and lack of strategic vision. We are also limited by the weakness of the explicitly socialist left and the disunity between left organizations. We find hope, however, in the unity built through the Revolutionary Work in Our Times Summer School.

We need strong revolutionary organizations that can bring together the social movement left with the membership of already existing left organizations. In order to lay the groundwork for that level of revolutionary organization, we identified four priorities: First, community-based organizing work in oppressed communities is the most important work that revolutionaries can be doing today. More revolutionaries need to be engaged in the work to build the power of oppressed people. Second, we have to promote the broadest possible development of revolutionary leadership rooted in oppressed communities, particularly in working class communities of color. Third, we need to continuously develop and refine a systematic understanding of the world we live in and what it will take to bring about the revolutionary transformation of society. We need spaces to develop and debate revolutionary theory and strategy, and forums to coordinate their implementation. Fourth, the constitution of a revolutionary left organization for the 21st century depends on the unification of the emergent left forces from social movements with socialist organizations (which need to build a higher level of inter-group unity in order to overcome past divisions).

We recently launched a new phase of study focused on developing left strategies to address the challenges and opportunities of the economic crisis and the "Obama era." This new focus has produced an overwhelming response and brought together more than 150 activists and organizers from around the city. We are combining both historical reflections on the high tide of resistance in New York during the Great Depression and assessments of our current conditions. This is a unique historical moment, and we hope these strategic dialogues will help us to develop the clarity we need to step up to the historic plate. We believe that if we can get more coordinated and strategic, our movements will look radically different ten years from now. ★

Note

1   These include the Catalyst Project and the School of Unity and Liberation (SOUL), two grassroots groups that run organizer training programs on anti-racist feminist practice, histories of organizing in communities of color, introduction to anti-capitalist politics, and strategies for contemporary revolutionary work.

[[[REVIEWS]]]

Solidarity and Responsibility

Katy Rose[1]

Candace Fujikane and Jonathan Y. Okamura (eds),
Asian Settler Colonialism: From Local Governance to
the Habits of Everyday Life in Hawai'i. **University of**
Hawaii Press, 2008.

The contemporary migrant justice movement has done an admirable job educating sectors of the Left and sustaining struggles to address the concerns of migrant workers. Grappling with questions of racism, workers' rights, imperialism and gender oppression, the migrant justice movement has encouraged us to expand our analyses of oppression and resistance.

But what do we understand about the relationship between the forced migration of people of colour into settler-colonial states and the coinciding displacement of Native peoples? What happens when immigrant groups successfully challenge oppressive conditions and gain collective power in settler-colonial states? Have struggles to attain civil rights and equity for people of colour within settler-colonial states contributed to the dispossession of indigenous people?

The archipelago of Hawai'i provides a helpful case study for examining these questions. Hawai'i is the homeland of the Kanaka Maoli. In 1778, they discovered British Captain James Cook anchored off Kaua'i. Cook's arrival began an era of conquest and genocide of the Kanaka Maoli that profoundly re-organized the islands' economic and social life. Of the missionaries that began arriving in 1820, it is often said that they "came to do good, and did very well." Along with new settlers from Europe and the United States, the missionaries' immediate descendents began large-scale sugar and pineapple operations. In order to supply the plantations, mills, and canneries with workers, *haole*[2] recruiters set off to various ports along the Pacific Rim, to places where war and imperialism had created intense pressures on impoverished populations to migrate to Hawai'i.

Waves of migrant workers arrived from Japan, China, Korea, and the Philippines. The conditions they faced in Hawai'i were brutal and racist. Organized resistance began almost immediately. Sugar workers on Kaua'i organized Hawai'i's first strike in 1841.

By the 1890s, a powerful new capitalist class backed by the US military, with its own geopolitical reasons for establishing a new military outpost in the Pacific, engineered the overthrow of the Hawaiian kingdom. Hawai'i became a territory of the United States. This arrangement granted wealthy business interests the protection of US power without the immigration restrictions inherent in outright US statehood. Nevertheless, by 1959, Hawai'i had become a state. Some of the strongest backers of statehood were Hawai'i-born Asian labourers who saw the move as a way to secure their rights as workers and full citizens. Statehood paved the way for the Asian working class to rise to prominence in local Democratic Party politics, the labor movement, and private enterprise.

Especially in light of mainstream media's account of Barack Obama's childhood on O'ahu, it is common to hear people describe Hawai'i as a multicultural paradise, an embodiment of the concept of "a nation of immigrants." Yet this completely elides the impact that colonialism and US hegemony have had on the Native population of Hawai'i. Between 1778 and 1900, the Kānaka Maoli[3] population fell by approximately 90 percent, from 800,000 to 37,000. Today, the Native people of Hawai'i fill the bottom ranks of critical social indices including longevity, income, incarceration rates, health statistics, and so on.[4] In response, Kanaka Maoli anti-colonialism has reasserted itself in a fierce struggle for independence and cultural survival.

The Hawaiian sovereignty movement arose during the earliest days of the US occupation of Hawai'i. Its modern era began in the late 1970s with a series of land struggles. These included the occupation of Kalama Valley on O'ahu and the attempt by Kānaka Maoli to reoccupy land in the island of Kaho'olawe that had been used for years as a military bombing range. The movement combines a variety of political strategies and tactics including direct action and legal battles in US and international courts.

While people of Asian ancestry – Hawai'i's majority – celebrate their history of resistance and carve out an identity distinct from (and sometimes hostile to) that of the continental US, a growing body of contemporary criticism interrogates both Asian-settler collusion with US power and the notion that Asian settlers have any more of a rightful claim to Hawai'i than do settlers from the US continent.

Asian Settler Colonialism: From Local Governance to the Habits of Everyday Life in Hawai'i is a new and controversial collection of essays by Asian settler and Kānaka Maoli scholars, activists, artists, and writers. It examines the relationship of Asian-settler society to the ongoing occupation of Hawai'i and suggests that people of Asian ancestry in Hawai'i establish a new and more self-conscious solidarity with the Native Hawaiian struggle for self-determination and sovereignty.

The editors divide the book into two sections, labeled "Native" and "Settler." As Candace Fujikane asserts, this reflects what she and others consider an appropriate positioning of settler allies in relation to Native peoples in struggle. Quoting from Imaikalani Kalahele's poem "Huli,"[5] which asks allies to "stand behind" Natives, and referring as well to Fanon's concept of a colonial world divided in two, Fujikane tells us that "the structure of the book reflects the structure of colonialism in Hawai'i and the lesson from Kalahele's poem. 'Native' comes first, 'Settler' follows and supports from behind."[6]

Much of the thinking in the multi-disciplinary volume draws inspiration from the critical analyses of the prominent Kanaka Maoli nationalist and academic Haunani-Kay Trask, whose ground-breaking essay "Settlers of Color and 'Immigrant' Hegemony: 'Locals' in Hawai'i" opens the first section of the volume.

Trask was one of the first activists to openly contest the liberatory discourse of "local" identity; the shorthand used to refer to Hawai'i-born descendants of the migrant plantation labourers. Exposing the term "local" as a gloss for "settler," Trask asserts that the children of Asian settlers "claim Hawai'i as their own, denying indigenous history, their long collaboration in our continued dispossession, and the benefits therefrom."[7]

While acknowledging the historical value of local identity in strengthening solidarity among migrant labour groups and their descendents, the contributors to Asian Settler Colonialism grapple honestly with Trask's challenge. This is done not to invalidate necessary struggles against racism but to build a solid foundation for social justice struggle based on the primacy of Native self-determination. The book emphasizes accountability, obligation, and action, rather than paralyzing guilt. As Fujikane puts it in her introduction to the collection:

> The status of Asians as settlers ... is not a question about whether they were the initial colonizers or about their relationship with white settlers. The identification of Asians as settlers focuses on their obligations to the indigenous peoples of Hawaii and the responsibilities that Asian settlers have in supporting Native peoples in their struggles for self-determination.[8]

More directly, adopting the term "Asian settler" is thought to shatter "US paradigms by forcing non-Natives to question our participation in sustaining US colonialism while making important political distinctions between Natives and non-Natives." As Fujikane explains, "I do not see the term as derogatory or, as some critics suggest, as pitting Natives against settlers." As contributor Dean Itsuji Saranillio states:

> The word "settler" is a means to an end. The goal is not to win in a game of semantics or to engage in name calling, but rather for settlers to have a firm understanding of our participation in sustaining US colonialism and then to support Native Hawaiians in achieving self-determination and the decolonization of Hawaii.[9]

The book argues that the organizing function of "local" identity in cementing class solidarity has lost its meaning in today's Hawai'i. It's a controversial position to people invested in organizing along class lines. Some veteran organizers of Asian ancestry have raised this concern and made the point that the appeal to class solidarity in Hawai'i does not preclude honest alliance building with the Hawaiian independence movement. For these critics, repositioning locals as "Asian settlers" needlessly alienates otherwise motivated people from engaging in anti-capitalist struggle. One friendly critic of the book's premise sardonically described to me the reception he would get if he greeted people in his working-class Filipino

community with a phrase like, "Greetings, fellow Asian settlers!"
Although nothing in the book promotes such an approach to
grassroots organizing, this particular organizer's point was clear: a
"settler" analysis was not going to move the people with whom he
worked into action.

One of the book's central themes is the critical difference
between anti-racist civil-rights-based movements and what
Fujikane calls "the uniqueness of indigenous struggle."[10] In light
of the Right's appropriation of the civil-rights framework and
the language of "colour-blindness" in its efforts to undermine
Native self-determination, it's important that we closely examine
the relationship between civil rights and indigeneity. Several
contributors take pains to illustrate that race is not the central
issue in the independence movement. This can seem confusing to
those who have tacitly absorbed the racialization of Kanaka Maoli.
However, while colonialism has imposed notions of blood quantum
and other racializing tools designed to wrest control of Native
lands, the central injustice for the Native Hawaiian movement is
the illegal overthrow of a sovereign state and the subsequent losses
inherent to that original act.

Two essays in particular take on the question of Asian settler
identity, anti-racist struggle, and the relationship of "civil rights"
to Native Hawaiians. Jonathan Okamura's "Ethnic Boundary
Construction in the Japanese American Community in Hawai'i"
deconstructs the neoconservative use of civil rights and the quest
for a "colour-blind" society, and considers the impact of ethnic
boundary construction in the dispossession of Native peoples.
Okamura explores recent legal challenges to various ethnically
based clubs and events – including the Americans of Japanese
Ancestry (AJA) Baseball League – and challenges to various
"race-based" entitlement programs for Native Hawaiians. From
the neo-conservative perspective, there's no difference between
these disparate institutions. Okamura points out that the result
is to distract attention from the significant political and economic
disparities that exist between all settlers and the Native people.
It also ignores the fact that Native people have a unique political
status as peoples under occupation that distinguishes them from
racial minorities seeking civil rights.

Dean Itsuji Saranillio looks more explicitly at the impact that
settler advances in gaining US citizen rights has had on Kānaka
Maoli. His essay "Colonial Amnesia: Rethinking Filipino 'American'
Settler Empowerment in the US Colony of Hawaii" carefully

compares the experience of colonization in the Philippines with that in Hawai'i and highlights the ways that Filipino migrants and their descendents have been systematically discouraged from supporting the Native struggle in Hawai'i. For Saranillio, "anti-racist projects that celebrate an American nationality must be rethought, for the grim reality is that US citizenship and 'success' as a good citizen is contingent upon the success of US settler colonization of indigenous peoples."[11]

Although the book tackles the political and economic conflict between Kānaka Maoli and Asian settlers, it also draws attention to the steady (if insufficient) history of settler solidarity with Native struggles. In particular, Ida Yoshinaga and Eiko Kosasa's "Local Japanese Women for Justice Speak out Against Daniel Inouye and the JACL" demonstrates the ways in which social justice activists of color in Hawai'i have linked race, class, anti-colonial, and Native struggles even in the face of tremendous pressure to uphold a united ethnic front. Yoshinaga and Kosasa revisit an op-ed they published in which they side with Hawaiian nationalist Mililani Trask against Daniel Inouye, Hawaii's powerful senior senator and Japanese-American World War II veteran, who is seen by many as the embodiment of immigrant success in the US. The op-ed was seen as a breach of ethnic solidarity and highlighted the courage required to challenge such a powerful figure.

As I write this, a battle over Native lands in Hawai'i is reaching a fever pitch in the courts, the statehouse, and the streets. At issue are 1.2 million acres of "ceded lands." These lands are the remaining Crown and Government lands of the Kingdom of Hawai'i. The United States seized these lands at the point of annexation and theoretically held them in trust for Native Hawaiians with the understanding that the question of sovereignty needed to be settled before the state could sell or transfer them. Some of the lands are undeveloped and pristine. Others include airports, harbours, military bases, and military-training facilities. Along with several other US states, the Governor of Hawai'i and her attorney general have convinced the US Supreme Court to hear an appeal of a recent Hawai'i Supreme Court ruling. This ruling essentially maintained the land in trust and reaffirmed the need to address the question of Native sovereignty. If the US Supreme Court hears the case, it's likely that the decision will not be favourable to Native Hawaiians and that the seized lands will be sold to the highest bidder in a massive act of dispossession.

The mythology of a gentle and willing transfer of Native lands to the US has clouded the central question of nationhood in the struggle over the "ceded" (seized) lands. It has created a rhetorical framework that emphasizes civil rights in opposition to greater state control over the lands. Although the central players on the State side of the battle are haole Republicans, the civil rights argument – that all races must be treated equally, and that treating Native Hawaiians differently hurts both them and the rest of the population – appeals to a multi-ethnic population for whom the route to justice depended heavily on the acquisition of civil rights under US law. As such, the State can also disingenuously propose that the sale of the lands will ease a budget crisis and provide for the needs of working people in Hawai'i through social services and affordable housing. In the process, the national question is thoroughly averted. Those that raise it are portrayed as divisive.

A concurrent and equally urgent fight concerns the Akaka Bill in the US Congress. This Democratic Party-supported bill would essentially recreate the Indian Reorganization Act of 1934 for Native Hawaiians and establish a semi-autonomous government. It's particularly dangerous because it would legally extinguish the sovereignty claims of the Kānaka Maoli, which remain unresolved even in the eye of US law. Needless to say, most Kānaka Maoli independence advocates are squarely against the bill and deeply concerned that Obama's election will assure its passage. In contrast, the majority of Hawai'i residents consider the Akaka Bill to be a fair and just approach to Native Hawaiian rights and fail to see the devastating consequences it will have for Kānaka Maoli national interests.

The great strength of Asian Settler Colonialism is that it offers social movement organizers a scholarly lens through which to view issues like the seized lands and the Akaka Bill. Although the question of "settler" terminology replacing "local" identity remains unresolved, the underlying premise of the book — that living on Native lands entails specific challenges and obligations — can help all of us to improve our solidarity with Native peoples' fight for decolonization.★

Notes

[1]   The author thanks Candace Fujikane, Dean Saranillio, Raymond Catania and Kyle Kajihiro for insights and education. All misrepresentations of the book, its contents or the surrounding political climate are the author's own.

[2]   *Haole* is a common Hawaiian-language term to refer to white settlers.

[3]   Kānaka Maoli is a Hawaiian word for Native Hawaiian.

[4]   David Stannard, "The Hawaiians: Health, Justice, and Sovereignty," *Asian Settler Colonialism: From Local Governance to the Habits of Everyday Life in Hawai'i.* University of Hawaii Press, 2008.

[5]   *Huli* a Hawaiian word meaning flip over or turn, as in revolution.

[6]   Candace Fujikane, "Introduction," Ibid.

[7]   Haunani-Kay Trask, "Settlers of Color and 'Immigrant' Hegemony: 'Locals' in Hawaii," Ibid.

[8]   Fujikane, Ibid.

[9]   Dean Itsuji Saranillio, "Colonial Amnesia: Rethinking Filipino "American" Settler Empowerment in the US Colony of Hawaii," Ibid.

[10]   Fujikane, Ibid.

[11]   Saranillio, Ibid.

Digging Up Autonomia

Frank Edgewick

Sylvère Lotringer, et al. (eds), *Autonomia:*
Post-Political Politics. **Semiotext(e), 2007.**

The original "movement of movements," Autonomia grew out of
the Italian student and worker mobilizations of 1968. It included
migrant workers, feminists, and the unemployed. In 1977, it
exploded into open revolt in the industrialized north of Italy. It
made important links between theory and action and marked a
major transition away from party structures towards mass anti-
authoritarianism.

Somewhere between an anthology and a cloud of news
clippings, Semiotexte's *Autonomia: Post-Political Politics* is an attempt
to conceptualize Autonomia as an event. A reprint of a 1980 edition
of the Semiotexte journal, *Autonomia* comprises three main parts,
Italian (post)-Marxist Autonomist theory, the arrest of its theorists,
and their critiques of the Leninist urban guerilla Red Brigades with
whom the prosecution conflated them. These are bookended by
introductions by Lotringer and Marazzi and a short comic from
the Autonomist journal *Metropoli*.

While the assemblage might have functioned to bring together
the event of Autonomia in 1980, today it's painfully obscure
even to those who are familiar with the movements, theorists,
and course of events it sets out to explore. Even when there are
indications of endnotes to explain the legions of minor officials and
demonstrations that get mentioned, they are often missing. Other
articles are cut to the point of nonsense. Oresto Scalzone's "From

Guaranteeism to Armed Politics" contains the section concerned with guaranteeism but armed struggle is nowhere to be found. Although it's not the only one, the contribution by American pacifist Judith Malina is simply a terrible piece of writing. While I understand the desire to publish a facsimile, it's painful to see that Semiotexte couldn't be bothered to correct the typos and fill in the blanks for readers to make the edition worthwhile.[1]

If you try to read it cover-to-cover, *Autonomia: Post-Political Politics* is a terrible book and a painful experience. However, if you're choosy, the collection can offer an interesting glimpse into the history of engaged theory. What's more, Autonomia's failures call into question our own anti-authoritarian practices. The trick is to avoid the articles that read like a cross between aged Reuters copy and wiretap transcripts, which are largely those dealing with the April 7th arrests of Autonomist theorists.

The reasons the movement was called "Autonomia" becomes clear in the course of the theoretical articles. The name denotes a state of affairs where something gives itself its own law or standard. In the first instance, it refers to those sections of the movement that were literally trying to build autonomous spaces outside of capitalism. In the second instance, it refers to the autonomy of workers from the "official worker's movement," the Italian Communist Party, and the parliamentary system. In the third instance, it refers to the autonomous productivity of the working class, which challenges capitalism to adapt to it. This point is significant, since it contradicts the Marxist orthodoxy that finds the working class beholden to the whims of capital. According to Autonomist theorist Mario Tronti, "the problem is already the other way around, and has been right from the start" (31).

While Marxism is the touchstone of Autonomist thought, Autonomia transformed several key concepts and, in the process, significantly altered class analysis and its relation to class struggle. Tronti's article "The Strategy of Refusal" addresses these transformations by considering the relationship between the class, its organization, and the revolution. According to Tronti, "when the class constitutes itself as a party, it is revolution in action" and that "the relationship Class-Party-Revolution is far tighter... than it is currently being presented, even by Marxists" (33-34). If we take this "tight" relationship to its logical conclusion, we can see that there is no interval between party, class, and revolution. For Tronti, the self-articulation of the working class as such is a revolutionary political achievement since it implies its breaking with its exploitative articulation by capital. Since the collapse of the temporal interval means that there can be no "planning for the revolution," Autonomia focuses on the self-valorization of the class through the organization of workers' refusal to submit to the logic of capital.

Each time the class articulates itself, capital must disrupt this composition with its own articulation or lose its dominance and die. According to Tronti, "increasing organization of exploitation, its continual reorganization at the very highest levels of industry and society are ... responses by capital to workers' refusal to submit" (31). The autonomous process of working class self-organization interacts with the process of capital but does not depend on it. For Tronti, working class power is "non-institutionalised political power" (32). Following this "tight" model to its conclusion, it becomes clear that class composition as a process is itself the field of political struggle.

Widening the political field in this way means that the entire social process – both inside and outside the factory – can be analysed in terms of its implications for class composition. In "The Tribe of Moles," Sergio Bologna describes how "the concepts of capital and class composition are far better suited to define the dynamic of class relations today as relations of power" (36). For Autonomia, not only is revolution a present-tense phenomenon, it is also a process that takes place in homes, schools, the media, and in the factory. These multiple fields of engagement mean that there are also multiple openings for revolutionary politics. These are the entry holes of the eponymous "Tribe of Moles" that digs away wherever capital articulates people into processes of exploitation.

Given the reoccupation of the large factories by the political system, Bologna proposes that it is the small factory that provides "the best terrain" for the mole to "dig once again" (50-51, 54). Since struggles are related to one another in the first instance only through their conflict with capital's productive articulation, Bologna argues that political potential rests in "a set of recompositional mechanisms that start, precisely, from a base of dishomogeneity" (51). Campaigns like wages for housework and the 150 hours paid study leave for factory workers made links across these varied fields, putting the factory, the university and the home in close contact, and so recombining them into a movement without homogenizing those based in each sector. At its best, the concept of class composition allows Autonomia to remain within the anti-capitalist tradition while diversifying its mode of struggle. It avoids falling into the ad hoc "common front" logic of a majority of political minorities because the struggle for class composition gives it unity.

Yet, maintaining class struggle at the centre of autonomist thought requires the sacrifice of an easily identifiable and homogenous protagonist. The dissolution of the hegemonic category "worker" marks a transition from socialist humanism to communist post-humanism. Although Negri's concept of "proletarian self-valorisation" entails a humanist project insofar as it considers direct valorization without passage through the commodity cycle, it ends by overturning the basis for humanist universality. This is because production itself fractures beyond recognition without the commodity form to constrain it. Autonomous social workers produce and realize their desires directly. They overflow the subjective limits of the "mass" worker and spill over into a schizo cluster of subjectivities as conceptualized by Deleuze and Guattari. Since socialist humanism is anchored by the universality of the social worker, the productive differentiation of social workers disrupts humanism.

Paolo Virno's "Dreamers of a Successful Life" provides an interesting account of Autonomia's movement toward the anti-humanist economy of desire envisioned by Deleuze and Guattari. He is critical of those who heap praise on the "new desires" for leisure, drugs, creative outlets, self-improvement, wellness and more, on the grounds that these desires are mistakenly imagined as outside of the productive cycle of capitalism itself. For Virno, "social needs no longer represent either the point of departure or the point of arrival for the process of production." Instead, "they constitute a 'middle term' in the route traveled [sic] by 'money as capital'" (115). Rather than denoting the "existential radicalness" of my own being, needs express the historical form of labour and are part of "that 'expanded reproduction' of the prevailing social relationships" (115). These diversifying needs are invested by capitalist articulation of the working class. However, Virno pushes it one step further. He writes:

> either needs are ordered by money and abstract labor, or they
> are filtered and arranged in a hierarchy in accordance with all
> the ramifications of the social aspect of the labor process, which
> is no longer measurable in terms of the law of value... from the
> reality of a broadened concept of labor stems a hierarchy of needs
> oriented toward emancipation, a hierarchy which is antithetical
> to the one mandated by the general equivalent (116).

For Virno, not only is desire itself not above suspicion, it must also be reworked as part of the revolutionary project. This requires that desire itself become an object of work and that it be subjected to hierarchical ordering on the basis of its use value for the project of self-valorization. This is in close proximity to the ethics of reconfigured desire in Deleuze and Guattari's work and the erotic ethics of techniques of the self in late Foucault, even while Virno maintains an explicitly revolutionary program.

Part of Virno's argument is that the revolutionary reorganization of needs requires a break with abstract labour and the general equivalent. It necessarily implies a break with capitalist economics, since money is the general equivalent and wage labour is human productive activity converted into its abstract monetary equivalent. In this way, Virno's analysis of desire leads him to reject economics and labour as contrary to revolutionary self-valorization. This is the point that Tronti arrives at through his macroanalysis of class struggle (where labour is the imposition of capital upon workers). It's not simply that capitalists wish to maximize their profit; labour is the condition for the existence of capitalists in the first place. Economics and labour are tools that rationalize and maintain capital's dependence on, and dominance over, the working class despite capital's ultimate subordination to workers (31). Consequently, for Negri, "proletarian self-valorisation is the power to withdraw from exchange value and the ability to reappropriate the world of use values" (66). At its simplest, Negri is referring to the worker's ability to take the afternoon off and enjoy the sunshine, a use value that can't be circulated to enrich capital. Pushed further, his thesis encompasses the refusal to allow potentially convertible use-values to be converted into exchange values, as when workers steal products rather than allowing them to be sold. At its logical conclusion, Autonomia implies a turn toward the direct appropriation of use-values.

The practical implications of this point are significant. The turn toward use-value demands a break with the social-democratic logic of collective bargaining, which poses demands in the language of exchange-value (pay for holidays, raises, insurance, etc.). In contrast, the emphasis on use-value allows for demands to be made that accord with subjects other than *homo oeconomicus* (including, at its threshold, group subjects of collective enjoyment). In this way, Autonomia's orientation to use-value ties together diverse forms of engagement including absenteeism, the autoreduction movement,[2] squats, the occupation of public space, and pirate radio. Each of these forms of engagement is objectively anti-capitalist because it breaks the relationship between money and use value that allows labour to be imposed on workers. They also work to integrate "non-workers" into the struggle, thus drawing the tribe of moles together to form a pack. As social workers, they recompose the new working class. As marginal phenomena, these forms of engagement are easily recovered by power structures. However, when they are linked together, they advance the process of self-valorization by joining people together in struggle while (at the same time) aiding an exodus from the labour relation.

Autonomia's analysis of exchange value and their emphasis on use value suggests a left criticism of socialism. Following from direct struggles over class-composition and opposition to the state as the means by which the working class becomes articulated exploited labour, Autonomia stands in opposition to socialism. From the point of view of left movements in North America, this might seem divisive and unreasonable. However, given the historical failure of socialism in the East and West, this line of reasoning deserves further consideration. Autonomia was a movement for communism; it implemented communism as its means of struggle. In contrast, socialism is a system concerned with the distribution of exchange value. It depends on the generalization of labour and state regulated class articulation to stabilize itself. This is antithetical to self-valorization, class composition, and post-economic cooperation. Socialized capital is still capital and behaves as such. While Marx suggested that socialism was an intermediate step from capitalism towards communism, Autonomia considered socialism an exploitative development of capitalism, contrary to communism, and considering the advanced stage of today's capitalism, argued for the viability of creating communism directly, here and now. Strategically, this means that we should not throw our energy behind centre-left strategies concerned with reforms. Instead, we need to work to make openings for the moles to begin digging once again.

Despite these important theoretical developments, Autonomia failed to achieve its goal. Exploitation was not replaced with self-organized communism, but rather was intensified. The Italian state made strategic use of the Red Brigades terrorist attacks in order to imprison tens of thousands of activists. But while the state's actions seriously impacted the movement, they cannot be viewed as the cause of Autonomia's failure. As an anti-authoritarian movement, Autonomia's vulnerability to this attack is a practical failure to disrupt the state. Given that state repression is now more effective than ever, the question with which we must concern ourselves is how Autonomia found itself in a position to be repressed at all. Paradoxically, it appears that Autonomia's failure arose precisely because it was so massive and vibrant. The movement's theorists attempted to find a unified language of universal expression so that the movement could bring together disparate social sectors in order to compose a new political subject. In the process, they became recognizable to the state as humanist subjects capable of expressing themselves. This represents a step backwards from class composition as social workers, a step back into the capitalist articulation of and domination over the working class. In so doing, they made themselves targets for arrest and imprisonment. Autonomia was still too intelligible, too universal, too much of a movement, and still too representational, mirroring the communications logic of the mass media. By launching so many books, magazines, newspapers, and radio stations, they allowed new noises to overtake new values.

This sombre note can be detected in Félix Guattari and Eric Alliez's contributions "The Proliferation of Margins" and "Hegel and the Wobblies." Although militants with Autonomia seem to have understood the pressing need to break with universality, it was never thoroughly put into practice. Similarly, Collective A / Traverso argue that Autonomia's failure arose from the fact that it obsessed over truth, opposing the obvious to the secret rather than seeking to become an imperceptible current or contagion. This is not a dry historical point since the contemporary theory of "Multitude" is a reworking of class composition and still works in much the same way. So too do many recent projects of the global extra-parliamentary left – from Gaza support to open borders activism to the renewal of labour organising. For the stunning successes and terrible failures of Autonomia, and our own organising, *Autonomia: Post-Political Politics* (or at least a portion of it) deserves careful consideration by contemporary anti-capitalists.★

Notes

[1]   Of course, an electronic facsimile of the original journal is available on-line at generation-online.org and text files of articles are available there and through marxists.org

[2]   "Autoreduction" is the term given to the process by which consumers set the price of commodities according to what they deem to be reasonable.

Voices of Freedom

Ernesto Aguilar

Matt Meyer (ed.), *Let Freedom Ring: A Collection of Documents from the Movement to Free US Political Prisoners*. PM Press, 2008.

In my office, stuffed in a green hanging file folder on four sheets of yellow legal paper is the original manuscript for "We Will Rise Again," Alvaro Luna Hernandez's manifesto on the Chicano Mexicano experience, his case, and the fight against colonialism. When I received "We Will Rise Again" from Alvaro about ten years ago, it was written in longhand, back and front, with calligraphic flourishes that are distinctly his. I typeset the original piece and laid it out as a pamphlet during the Barrio Defense Committee's intense struggle to win Alvaro's freedom. That manifesto is now a part of *Let Freedom Ring: A Collection of Documents from the Movement to Free US Political Prisoners*.

Tragically, Alvaro's campaign waned as the brutally slow criminal justice system did what it does best: drain time, resources, energy, and hope from its victims and those around them. So many initiatives meet this same fate: they get ground into dust, and years vanish in the blink of an eye. But those years were witness to thousands of committed individuals that sought, in large ways and small, to gain freedom for political prisoners. Some stayed, others moved on, yet the passion for liberty remains strong. If nothing else, the continuous revitalization of movements against capitalism and for national liberation around the planet is testament to *that*.

No other compilation on the struggles of political prisoners is as extensive as *Let Freedom Ring*, which sets it aside as outstanding. Scores of previously released documents are printed alongside newer writings. From tracts handed out at meetings to pamphlets distributed through communities, pieces that were seemingly lost to time and forgotten in personal collections are diligently repackaged for posterity. In that sense, *Let Freedom Ring* is as much a tribute to those unknown individuals who worked anonymously behind the scenes as it is a presentation of the writers and captives that make up the public face of the fight to free political prisoners.

If you've been involved in political prisoner and prison abolition activism – and even if you haven't – *Let Freedom Ring* is both touching and remarkable. Editor Matt Meyer manages to compile dozens of documents into a book that gives coherence to an important but often invisible movement. Rather than enlisting writers to document the movement, debate particular facets, or reflect on various periods, Meyer chooses instead to publish writings collected from the last generation of strugglers. The authors in *Let Freedom Ring* will look familiar: Dhoruba bin Wahad, Laura Whitehorn, Leonard Peltier, Mumia Abu-Jamal, and others are featured, albeit in pieces that in numerous instances have been published in other forms. Rather than being a drawback, having the writings of so many political prisoners who are able to reflect on vital moments like the founding of the now-defunct political prisoner liberation formation Freedom Now! and its successor, the Jericho Movement, provides a rich context for considering the very idea of what it means to be a political prisoner. Never has such a treatment happened so holistically; never has it been afforded the 800 plus pages that *Let Freedom Ring* has given it.

Dan Berger kicks off the book with one of the best reviews of the history of political militancy I've read. Known for documenting the radical political struggles of groups like the Weather Underground Organization, Berger introduces the reader to the movements from which political prisoner populations have historically been derived and explains the central political tenets of these movements. Commenting on the Black Panther Party and Black Liberation Army, Fuerza Armadas de Liberación Nacional and Republic of New Afrika, Berger covers some expected terrain. But he also considers movements and groups that often get overlooked such as Los Siete de la Raza, the George Jackson Brigade, and insurgencies led by theories of revolutionary nonviolence. Turning his attention to those behind bars, Berger also relates the stories of some of the best-known political prisoners. For those seeking a discerning introduction to these matters, Berger's essay is a good place to start.

Although *Let Freedom Ring* has an ambitious scope, Meyer manages to pull it off. It is more than a series of lamentations about prison conditions, cases, and legalese. Instead, it highlights what many organizers consider central to understanding what it means to be a political prisoner. For white anti-imperialists and Black nationalists alike, every individual considered in the volume was and is motivated by a commitment to social justice, self-determination, and revolution from the inside and out. Because of the dour iconography of cages and fists that dot the landscape of political prisoner movements, the passion and devotion of political prisoners to these collective ideals is often lost. Not here. Meyer balances writings of pain in prison with words about the struggles of today.

If the book has a weakness, it arises in its account of the connection of political prisoner activism to broader social justice movements. How are organizers on the outside integrating the political prisoner movement into a broader agenda concerned with criminalization and oppression? And where, if anywhere, is such work happening successfully? While most of the pieces in the book are historical hip-checks, fierce reminders of white supremacy, occupation and resistance, not nearly enough ink is given to how the overall commitment of the prisoners themselves is (or could be) effectively connected to contemporary political organizing. In my experience as an organizer, political prisoner questions have often been treated parochially and isolated (sometimes for confusing reasons) from the broader question of criminal justice. And while a focus on political prisoners may have threatened to overshadow a particular campaign, it would at least have brought important names and history into a new light.

To its credit, *Let Freedom Ring* does its best to talk about liberation movements even when their connections to the struggle to free political prisoners may not be so clear. The book travels along a winding and wonderful radical road. David Gilbert, an important yet consistently overlooked political thinker, has many writings here. His essay, "Some Lessons from the 1960s," should be required reading for every movement activist. Marilyn Buck's memorable politics, poetry, and prose grace many pages. Eve Goldberg and Linda Evans' investigation of the prison-industrial complex is as relevant now as when it was written over a decade ago. The United States government's crimes against the black liberation movement and its targeting of US civil rights organizers are discussed alongside the Puerto Rican independence tendency, radical direct-action environmentalism, and the San Francisco Eight.

At many turns, *Let Freedom Ring* goes far beyond its stated focus on political prisoners and delves into matters like health care, institutional racism, and military resistance. When stepping out, some notable omissions become evident. Among these are the role that groups like the Crossroad Support Network played in popularizing political prisoner issues within the New Afrikan Independence Movement and elsewhere, and the work of the late Jim Campbell and the Bulldozer Collective. The latter published *Prison News Service*, the Canadian prisoners' newspaper which regularly featured contributions by many of the writers included in *Let Freedom Ring* alongside debates on key ideological issues.

Given the prominence of anarchists and anarchist organizing in *Let Freedom Ring*, it's surprising that Lorenzo Kom'boa Ervin – a former Black Panther who actively organized around criminal justice and political prisoner affairs and who had a profound impact on the anti-authoritarian milieu in the early 1990s – gets virtually no mention at all. Whether or not you agreed with Kom'boa, and whether or not you recall his rows with groups like the Love & Rage Revolutionary Anarchist Federation, his contributions to political prisoner and prison abolition debates cannot be overlooked as it is in this compilation.

Activists need to consider how criminal justice reform, political prisoner efforts, and prison abolition find common ground, where they succeed, and where they can learn from one another. Although political prisoner activists come from diverse movements, too few analyze what worked in those movements and apply it to political prisoner engagements. When I was involved in the Anarchist Black Cross, there were many conflicts about the status of these connections. This seemed to be a weakness of many other groupings as well. Developing a coherent vision that recognizes that our relationships to multiple struggles are a benefit rather than a betrayal seems necessary; exploring how to *do* that is terrain we still need to cross.

Similarly, it's important for us to consider the status of those captives who are not explicitly affiliated with broader political movements. Are we valuing "politicized" prisoners in a way that benefits the larger movement? Nowhere in *Let Freedom Ring* do we find a critical examination, for example, of the struggle for the soul of the Almighty Latin King and Queen Nation or the contributions of Sanyika Shakur, the controversial former Eight Tray Gangster Crips leader whose incarceration led to his politicization and the authorship of *Monster: Autobiography of an LA Gang Member*. This is significant, since the book brought New Afrikan ideals to mainstream audiences in the 1990s. Although Berger name-drops Shakur in his contribution, the overall political significance of these movements remain unexplored. In an era when youth culture's conception of political prisoners has been shaped by Tony Yayo and the late Pimp C, how can we justify our failure to put names like Sundiata Acoli back on the radar of popular consciousness?

The decision to publish the pieces from the eras in which they occurred gives *Let Freedom Ring* a sense of urgency. However, the book misses an important mark by restricting itself to its rearview mirror look at the movement. Rank-and-file prison abolition and political prisoner movement organizers need to grapple with why we seem to be in the same place now as we were when many of today's political prisoners were first incarcerated. These courageous souls have aged behind bars. Some have died. And only a precious few have been released. Although there have been victories, the movement remains largely unknown to most left-wing political activists. To the broader public, these prisoners are nearly invisible.

These questions are incredibly complex and it's only through careful consideration that we can avoid falling back on recriminating attitudes. In fairness, *Let Freedom Ring* tackles a few of these questions, but what's missing is a satisfying interpretation. As a documentary collection, perhaps this isn't the place for that work. Nevertheless, many newcomers to the struggle won't notice the gaps, which only increases Meyer's obligation to explore them.

Meyer describes *Let Freedom Ring* as a resource guide. But it's more than that: it is the chronicle the political prisoner movement has needed for a long time. By republishing works that have for too long languished in hanging file folders, Meyer encourages us to recommit to the struggle for those who have languished far too long behind bars. ★

Highly Mediated

DT Cochrane

Robert W. McChesney, *The Political Economy of Media*. Monthly Review Press, 2008.

As with all things under the control of capital, the mainstream media aims for profitability. Under the current dominant model, media profitability depends on advertising, which fosters an important relationship between media owners and the rest of Big Business. According to Internal Revenue Service data, total US spending on advertising now tops 250 billion dollars per year and the largest 0.04 percent of corporations are responsible for 50 percent of that spending. But what makes the media an especially unique asset for capitalism is that it serves as the primary source for disseminating political, cultural, and economic ideas. Media-controlling corporations play a direct role in shaping how people understand social relations. They police the boundaries of social discourse to protect and legitimize the capitalist status quo.

Neither the media's function as a profitable asset nor its role as gatekeeper of social discourse can be ignored. For this reason, a radical critique of the media must identify how it functions on various levels as an integral part of capitalism. Further, radicals must establish their own relationships to media, given our need to participate in social discourse as part of efforts to instigate change. On this score, Robert McChesney's *The Political Economy of Media* both succeeds and fails. His analysis of the political economic history of the media system is excellent; he makes clear that the contemporary media system coevolved with monopoly capital and is not merely in need of reform. Yet, when considering resistance to the media system, he focuses on battles that are largely aimed at holding back corporate media advances rather than rolling them back as part of a larger struggle against capital. It's not that McChesney's ideas about "resistance" are undesirable in and of themselves, but rather that they exclude the very anti-capitalist critique his own historical and political economic analysis would seem to demand. McChesney rightly derides analyses that try to treat the media like any other facet of capital, but he then tries to elevate media reform above every other anti-capitalist struggle. Anti-capitalists need to acknowledge the role of media reform. However, this means approaching reforms with the aim of undermining and moving beyond capital.

Capital's interest in the media's protective function should be obvious. Nevertheless, in the US we continually hear claims that the news media has a "left/liberal bias" (with the term liberal itself having been twisted to denote anything moderately socially progressive). Defenders of the media system weigh the charge of liberal bias against the charge of right-wing bias and conclude that the debate itself is proof that media remains as neutral and objective as possible. Activists are often drawn into this debate and join the call for balanced news coverage and a reduction in ownership concentration.

The media's "conservative bias" and the increasing concentration of media outlets are both worrisome. However, if the mainstream media is wholly beholden to capitalist owners and advertisers, are balance and ownership diversity all we need? This question demands that we ask and answer some others. What, precisely, is the relationship between media as a means of communication and the accumulation drive of capital? How should anti-capitalists engage with mainstream media and its "alternative" counterparts? Does our critique of capitalism require a distinct critique of capitalist media? And can radicals support demands for reform without becoming merely reformist? In considering questions such as these, McChesney's analysis digs beneath the glittering distortion of surface impressions to consider how the contemporary media system is the product of the process of capitalist accumulation and not merely its unwilling hostage.

McChesney is well known and much praised among left-liberals. His work has appeared in *The Nation*, *The Progressive*, *In These Times*, *Z*, and *Monthly Review* and he has collaborated with Edward Herman and Ellen Meiksins Wood. Noam Chomsky,

Howard Zinn, Ralph Nader, and Jesse Jackson have all written blurbs for his books. Weary of his celebrity status on the left, I began to read *The Political Economy of Media* with an admittedly jaundiced eye. Nonetheless, I can say that the book provides a good introduction to McChesney's work, an informative explanation of how contemporary professional journalism coevolved with commercialization, a wide-ranging critical assessment of mainstream media, and an interesting overview of recent media reform campaigns. The book is not without its faults, though, and these begin with a misleading presentation of its own contents.

Although it's unclear from the title, *The Political Economy of Media* is actually a collection of previously published essays, rather than a single text of new material. Only one chapter – ten pages out of 589 – contains material that's entirely unique to this book. As a collection of essays, the book lacks the flow and cohesion of a single text. For example, a chapter on Noam Chomsky's critique of neoliberalism inexplicably follows a chapter on the increasingly blurred line between editorial and commercial content. The lack of transparency about the book's status as a collection of essays is misleading and violates a basic courtesy to the reader. Let's hope that subsequent editions add the subtitle "Collected Essays."

To be fair, many of the essays were first published in obscure anthologies and may be unfamiliar to many McChesney readers. For those less familiar with his work, *The Political Economy of Media* provides a comprehensive overview of an important body of research, bringing together McChesney's academic and popular works, with articles that previously appeared in peer-reviewed journals such as *Journalism Studies* and *Journal of Communication* alongside those from explicitly partisan sources such as *Monthly Review* and *Socialist Register.* As a collection of essays, it's easy to jump around and read the chapters that are of greatest interest.

The essays are readable and easily understood. McChesney does not weigh the reader down with jargon and even the essays originally written for scholarly journals are free of cumbersome academic vernacular. Because the book is not a single, original text, it cannot be reviewed in terms of a central argument carried throughout. Instead, I will focus here on what I think McChesney does best: exploring the political economic history of media in the US and the role of business in media's development; and what he appears to consider most important: the US media reform movement in which he has played a large role.

Under capitalism, mainstream media are predominantly commercial enterprises. For McChesney, this is the starting point for a political economy of media. Where most scholarly research on media and communications accepts as given the media's commercial nature and its integration into capitalism, political economists of media do not. For them, ownership structures and commercial interests are important for understanding media content. This critical stance provokes political economists of media to consider how the media interact with other dynamics of capitalism such as racism, sexism, and militarism. McChesney claims that this perspective leads political economists of media to adopt an advocacy position concerned with enhancing democracy.

For McChesney, a functioning democracy depends on a vibrant and healthy media system. The first line of the first essay, "The problem of journalism" makes McChesney's position clear: "Democratic theory generally posits that society needs a journalism that is a rigorous watchdog of those in power and who want to be in power, can ferret out truth from lies, and can present a wide range of informed positions on the important issues of the day" (25). No postmodern advocate of journalism as storytelling or fetishist of changing technology, McChesney maintains a classically liberal position on the media as a mechanism of public dialogue and opinion formation.

However, as McChesney explains, today's "professional journalist" striving to be neutral, non-partisan, and "objective," is not what Enlightenment-era liberal theorists and politicians had in mind when they advocated for a free press. It is insufficient to claim that corporate interests infringe upon the objectivity previously enjoyed by the free press since the very ideas of neutrality and objectivity were actually products of the commercialization of media.

Exploring the political economic history of media makes it clear that contemporary media has not suddenly become hostage to intensifying commercial interests. Rather, it has evolved and grown as an integral component of those interests. Prior to the concentration of media outlets in the late 19th and early 20th centuries, the range of opinion was broader, more diverse, and highly partisan. People could immerse themselves in a sea of explicitly one-sided opinions. Viewed from McChesney's classic liberal position, this is desirable since it fostered public debate and allowed citizens to form their own opinions rather than adopt those favoured by elites.

As the press became monopolized, its overt partisanship became more problematic. Concentration resulted in fewer owners and fewer opinions. As a result, the public became increasingly distrustful of media. Criticism of media's capitalist bias became widespread. Publishers realized that public confidence had to be restored if newspapers were to remain profitable. Consequently, according to McChesney, they sacrificed "their explicit political power to lock in their economic position" (29). In order to do this, they established schools of journalism to train generations of "professionals." The ethics of this profession called for a separation between the press's commercial interests and its editorial content. The journalist was expected to suppress value judgments and simply "report the facts." With these guiding principles in place, the previous generation's press diversity was made to seem superfluous since the public would be offered the unvarnished truth. Although they are not commercial enterprises in the ordinary sense, even state or publicly funded media institutions such as the CBC, PBS, or the BBC have fallen into this model of the professional journalist. McChesney's critique remains valid for all mainstream media and pre-empts attempts to acquit public broadcasters on the basis that not-for-profit status somehow ensures diverse coverage.

According to McChesney, "professional journalism" instituted biases in the press. These included an over-reliance on "official sources" – government officials, experts, and other professionals – and story selection that favoured commercial interests. However, despite these problems, McChesney notes that until the 1970s journalists had a degree of autonomy and could at least choose and investigate stories. Now, with declining newsroom budgets and increasing concentration, the situation is getting worse. Today's journalists are often little more than glorified stenographers to official sources. Meanwhile, the scope of "official" sources has been broadened to include representatives of business, while controversy is feigned by wallowing in the muck of celebrity misdeeds rather than by uncovering the crimes of business and government. Twenty-four hour news channels proliferate but journalism is increasingly hard to find.

Alongside this history of contemporary journalism and commerce, McChesney explores radical 20th century critiques of mainstream media. He notes that this history is often unknown in the US, where a powerful mythology surrounds the press. Americans are told that their media system is the envy of the world because of its neutrality, nonpartisanship, and objectivity, and because its freedom is guaranteed by the Constitution. A history of critique can hardly co-exist with such a sacred institution. However, this history of critique coincides with most Americans' gnawing doubts about the media's commercialism and their distrust of its coverage. According to McChesney, even journalists are beginning to question and criticize corporate control of the press. As with the high point of press criticism during the early 20th century, today's media operate in a context of increasing concentration, greater public awareness of commercial influence, and the emergence of alternative media projects.

Unfortunately, these parallels are as depressing as they are inspiring. After all, the earlier era's critique included an explicit and widespread indictment of capitalism. McChesney writes that all of the challengers in the 1912 US presidential election – Eugene V. Debs, Theodore Roosevelt, and Woodrow Wilson – criticized the press for having a capitalist bias. This would be unthinkable today. What's more, even with radical criticism, the reforms that came out of that era ultimately served to strengthen the capitalist press. Given the contemporary media's pedigree as a product of commercial interests, mere reforms are unlikely to produce the conditions necessary for a genuine democracy.

Unfortunately, reforms are all McChesney has to offer. He calls for increased support for media workers, alternative press, and labour/left think tanks. He recommends lobbying efforts to change government policy. He declares that the "objective is a more diverse and competitive commercial system with a significant nonprofit and noncommercial sector" (391). Essentially, McChesney calls for a return to the partisan era that preceded the commercial takeover even though partisanship itself failed to prevent the initial conglomeration. Making a fetish of that era's partisanship is especially dangerous in light of the fuel it added to the sectarianism that immolated radical movements. Partisanship helped to derail Debs's inspirational presidential campaign and bolstered labour's misguided support for Wilson. Although the reforms advocated by McChesney are desirable, it's hard to see how they would provoke sweeping social change unless they are incorporated into explicitly anti-capitalist organizing.

To be sure, McChesney has done much to highlight how commercial interests perniciously impact the press in both practice and content. He acknowledges the need to connect media criticism to the critique of capitalism. Nevertheless, he stops short of exploring how the media reform movement can become explicitly anti-capitalist. Instead, he maintains his classically liberal posture and assures us that, if media reform "is debated in the light of day, there will be progressive outcomes" (497).

According to McChesney, this debate is happening and the media reform movement is becoming larger and more powerful. As evidence, in a chapter entitled "The Escalating War Against Corporate Media," he describes the 2003-2004 fight against the Federal Communications Commission (FCC) attempt to relax ownership restrictions. However, while the movement managed to stop a policy change favourable to the corporate media, it failed at its stated aim of strengthening ownership restrictions. At best, the campaign was an "escalating defense against corporate media." This is not to deny the movement's real achievements. However, if these achievements are not placed in a radical anti-capitalist context, they become reformist and risk being rolled back or transformed in ways favourable to capitalist interests. For McChesney, "if changing media is left until 'after the revolution,' there will be no revolution" (461). In response, it suffices to note that, if the revolution is left until after we change the media, there will be no revolution.

Creating a more humane political economy demands a massive effort on every front. It means confronting every institution controlled by the capitalist elite. This struggle demands that we understand all of the institutions under capitalist control, and few provide a better understanding of the capitalist media than McChesney. Reforms like those sought by the McChesney-founded Free Press can be important steps in the process of confrontation. However, the reform of a single institution cannot produce the sufficient conditions for sweeping social change. This is especially true if activists seeking reform allow themselves to be co-opted by electoral politics. Co-optation of this sort remains all too common and was on full display during last year's Free Press organized National Conference for Media Reform, where a number of speakers openly endorsed Obama. This is not to say that the media reform movement should completely abandon electoral politics. Instead, it is a call to recognize that activists seeking reform will have a far greater impact when backed by a radical critique than if they are drawn to enthusiastically endorse one corporate funded candidate over another. For all of his attentiveness, McChesney neglects to read the fine print. There, it is written that reforms, if they are to be successful, must be the caption on the big picture – a humane post-capitalist society. ★

BASICS
FREE COMMUNITY NEWSLETTER

BASICS Free Community Newsletter is a rapidly growing grassroots newspaper movement in Canada made up of workers, youth, students, and progressive people fighting for people's power and self-determination in our communities, schools, and workplaces.

We are self-funded and rely on the contributions of our organization's members and supporters to get thousands of copies of BASICS right to peoples' doors.

You can help build our work by taking out a subscription of our newspaper or by making a donation:
$30 - 1 Year (6 issues) or $50 - 2 Years (12 issues)

Send a cheque or money order to the address below to subscribe or donate, or feel free to contact us through email to inquire about various forms of online payment (PayPal or email money transfer)

Basics Free Community Newsletter
P.O. Box 97001
R.P.O. Roncesvalles
Toronto, ON M6R 3B3
Email: basics.canada@gmail.com or **Website**: basicsnewsletter.blogspot.com

If you are serious about becoming a community organizer associated with BASICS or distributing BASICS in your area, workplace, or school, please contact us at the email above.

[[CONTRIBUTOR NOTES]]

Ernesto Aguilar is a media worker whose efforts have included work with the Anarchist Black Cross Federation and Network, as well as founding the Anarchist People of Color email list from which the APOC tendency emerged. He is based in Houston, Texas.

Dan Berger is the author of *Outlaws of America: The Weather Underground and the Politics of Solidarity* (AK Press, 2006). Although he was born in the 1980s, he currently spends most of his time in the 1970s: he is co-editing a book and writing a dissertation about radical American social movements in that period.

John Clarke was born in London, England where his first political activity involved organizing with other school students in the early 1970s. He was later active in trade union struggles as a hospital worker. In 1976, he moved to London, Ontario, took a job in the local Westinghouse plant and become a shop steward with the United Electrical Workers. Laid off in 1982, he helped form the London Union of Unemployed Workers and, in 1990, moved to Toronto to become an organizer with the newly formed Ontario Coalition Against Poverty. He has been with OCAP ever since.

DT Cochrane's research interests revolve around the intra-capitalist accumatory struggle and how resistance movements can inject themselves into the process. He is a PhD student at York University.

Aidan Conway is an editor of *Upping the Anti* and a PhD student at York University.

Chris Dixon, originally from Alaska, is a longtime anti-authoritarian activist, writer and educator, and a PhD student at the University of California at Santa Cruz. He lives in Sudbury, Ontario, Atikameksheng Anishnawbek Territory, where he organizes with Sudbury Against War and Occupation. Contact him at chrisd@resist.ca.

Frank Edgewick is an Ottawa-based labour and community organizer who is currently exploring concepts and strategies for social change beyond the political.

Gary Kinsman is an anti-capitalist and queer liberation activist who lives in Sudbury and is an advisory board member of *Upping the Anti*. He teaches sociology at Laurentian University and is a member of Sudbury Against War and Occupation.

Shourideh Molavi is a MA student at York University. For the past 4 years, she has worked with the Palestinian community in Gaza City, Jerusalem, and Haifa. Her current post is at MADA al-Carmel – the Arab Center for Applied Social Research, an independent research institute located in Haifa, Israel.

Shiri Pasternak is a second year PhD student in the Planning department of the University of Toronto and the coordinator Barriere Lake Solidarity – Toronto.

Katy Rose considers our mutually assured liberation to be her life's work. She does her best to build up social and economic justice while standing up to imperialism, capitalism and oppression. Born and raised in California, she now lives on the island of Kaua'i, Hawai'i, with her husband and two teenage sons, where she works in a public high school and engages in local grassroots organizing with the Kaua'i Alliance for Peace and Social Justice. She also produces a public affairs radio program on Kaua'i community radio, which highlights radical grassroots organizing in Hawai'i and beyond.

Erik Ruin is a Michigan-raised, Philly-based printmaker, shadow-puppeteer, and occassional editor of various publications, most recently the anthology *Realizing the Impossible: Art Against Authority* (with Josh MacPhee, AK Press, 2007). As a visual artist, he frequently works collaboratively with other artists or with activist campaigns, and has created imagery for organizations engaged in work ranging from urban farming to housing cooperatives to prisoner advocacy. In 2006, he banded together with twelve other radical artists to create the Justseeds Visual Resistance Artists Cooperative as a national network to distribute work and foster creative alliances with social movements. Some of his print work is viewable at: http://www.justseeds.org/artists/erik_ruin

Suzy Subways is editor of the Solidarity Project, an internet publication about HIV prevention justice organizing from the Community HIV/AIDS Mobilization Project (CHAMP). She writes about AIDS activism for New York City's *Indypendent* and Philadelphia's *defenestrator*. Previously an editor at *POZ* magazine, she was also a member of the Love and Rage Revolutionary Anarchist Federation and a founding member of the Student Liberation Action Movement (SLAM) in New York City. She lives in Philadelphia, where she is part of the Coalition to Save the Libraries.

COPIES OF UPPING THE ANTI NUMBER TWO
ARE AVAILABLE FOR $10 EACH INCLUDING MAILING COSTS.

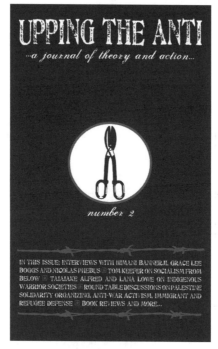

UPPING THE ANTI

...a journal of theory and action...

number 2

IN THIS ISSUE: INTERVIEWS WITH HIMANI BANNERJI, GRACE LEE BOGGS AND NICOLAS PHEBUS ® TOM KEEFER ON SOCIALISM FROM BELOW ® TAIAIAKE ALFRED AND LANA LOWE ON INDIGENOUS WARRIOR SOCIETIES ® ROUND TABLE DISCUSSIONS ON PALESTINE SOLIDARITY ORGANIZING, ANTI-WAR ACTIVISM, IMMIGRANT AND REFUGEE DEFENSE ® BOOK REVIEWS AND MORE...

★INTERVIEWS★
Himani Bannerji: The Politics of Race and Class.
Grace Lee Boggs: Revolution as a New Beginning Part 2.
Nicolas Phebus: The Strike of the General Assemblies.

★ARTICLES★
Tom Keefer: Marxism, Anarchism & Socialism From Below.
Taiaiake Alfred & Lana Lowe: Indigenous Warrior Societies.

★ROUNDTABLES★
Perspectives on Palestine Solidarity Organizing with Mordecai Briemberg,
Paul Burrows, Samer Elatrash, Adam Hanieh & Rafeef Ziadah.
Anti-War Activism with Chris Arsenault, Honor Brabazon & Jessie X., Mike
DesRoches, Derrick O'Keefe, Andrea Schmidt and George 'Mick' Sweetman.
Non-Status (Im)migrant Justice in Canada with
Sarita Ahooja, Harsha Walia and Sima Zerehi.

★BOOK REVIEWS★
Adrian Harewood on *A View of Freedom* by Dave Austin and Alfie Roberts
Kirat Kaur on *Ten Thousand Roses* by Judy Rebick.
Karl Kersplebedeb on *Caliban and the Witch* by Silvia Frederici
Tyler McCreary on *Settlers* by J. Sakai.

SEND CHEQUES TO "UTA PUBLICATIONS"
998 BLOOR ST. WEST, P.O. BOX 10571, TORONTO ON CANADA M6H 4H9
OR ORDER ONLINE AT WWW.UPPINGTHEANTI.ORG

COPIES OF UPPING THE ANTI NUMBER THREE
ARE AVAILABLE FOR $10 EACH INCLUDING MAILING COSTS.

★INTERVIEWS★
Aijaz Ahmad: The Anti-Imperialism of Our Times.
William Robinson: Latin America vs. Global Capitalism.

★ARTICLES★
AK Thompson: Making Friends with Failure.
Isabel MacDonald: Haiti: Adventures in Colonialism.
RJ Maccani: The Zapatistas: Enter the Intergalactic.
Jen Plyler: How To Keep On Keeping On.

★ROUNDTABLES★
Six Nations Struggles with Tom Keefer, Brian Skye, and Jan Watson.
OCAP Activists discuss Six Nations Solidarity Work with
AJ Withers, Stefanie Gude and Josh Zucker.

★BOOK REVIEWS★
Scott Neigh on *Sociology for Changing the World* by Caelie Frampton et al.
Yutaka Dirks on *Outlaws of America* by Dan Berger.
Sharmeen Khan on *Autobiography of a Blue-Eyed Devil* by Inga Muscio.

SEND CHEQUES TO "UTA PUBLICATIONS"
998 BLOOR ST. WEST, P.O. BOX 10571, TORONTO ON CANADA M6H 4H9
OR ORDER ONLINE AT WWW.UPPINGTHEANTI.ORG

COPIES OF UPPING THE ANTI NUMBER FIVE
ARE AVAILABLE FOR $10 EACH INCLUDING MAILING COSTS.

IN THIS ISSUE: SUNERA THOBANI ON CANADIAN FEMINISM ✱ GORD HILL
ON INDIGENOUS ANTI-COLONIALISM ✱ MICHAEL HARDT ON PERSPECTIVES
OF RESISTANCE ✱ MACDONALD STAINSBY ON THE ALBERTA TAR SANDS
✱ CAELIE FRAMPTON ON STUDENT ORGANIZING AND THE CFS ✱ RAMI
EL-AMINE AND MICHAEL STAUDENMAIER ON ISLAM, FASCISM AND THE LEFT
✱ POLITICAL PRISONER ROUNDTABLE WITH ASHANTI ALSTON, SETH HAYES,
SUSAN TIPOGRAPH, AND SARA FALCONER ✱ BOOK REVIEWS AND MORE...

★INTERVIEWS★
Sunera Thobani: The Fight for Feminism.
Gord Hill: The Indigenous Tradition of Resistance.
Michael Hardt: From the Perspective of Resistance.

★ARTICLES★
Macdonald Stainsby: Tar Sands and Oil Production in Western Canada.
Caelie Frampton: A Radical Critique of the CFS.
Michael Staudenmaier & Rami El-Amine: Anti-Semitism, Islamophobia
and the Left – The Three Way Fight Debate.

★ROUNDTABLES★
Political Prisoner Roundtable with
Ashanti Alston, Robert 'Seth' Hayes, Susan Tipograph and Sara Falconer.

★BOOK REVIEWS★
Chris Harris on *We Will Return in the Whirlwind* by Muhammad Ahmad.
Anna Feigenbaum on *Pacifism as Pathology* by Ward Churchill
and *How Nonviolence Protects the State* by Peter Gelderloos.
Matthew N. Lyons on *The Past Didn't Go Anywhere: Making Resistance
to Anti-Semitism Part of All of Our Movements* by April Rosenblum.

SEND CHEQUES TO "UTA PUBLICATIONS"
998 BLOOR ST. WEST, P.O. BOX 10571, TORONTO ON CANADA M6H 4H9
OR ORDER ONLINE AT WWW.UPPINGTHEANTI.ORG

COPIES OF UPPING THE ANTI NUMBER SEVEN
ARE AVAILABLE FOR $10 EACH INCLUDING MAILING COSTS.

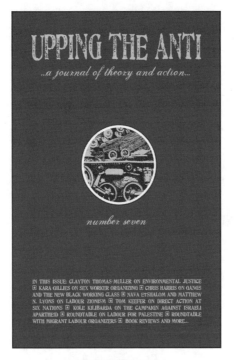

★INTERVIEWS★
Clayton Thomas-Müller: Just Environmentalism?
Kara Gillies: Sex Work and the State.
Chris Harris: Building to Building, Hood to Hood.

★ARTICLES★
Nava EtShalom and Matthew N. Lyons: The Story of Labour Zionism.
Tom Keefer: Direct Action, Six Nations, and the Struggle in Brantford.
Kole Kilibarda: The BDS Movement in Canada.

★ROUNDTABLES★
Labour Solidarity for Palestine with
Dave Bleakney, Iliam Burbano, Andy Griggs, and Jenny Peto.
Migrant Labout Organizing with Evelyn Calugay,
Tess Tesalona, Adriana Paz, Aylwin Lo, and Chris Ramsaroop.

★BOOK REVIEWS★
Neil Balan on *In Defense of Lost Causes* by Slavoj Žižek.
Alejandro de Acosta on *Infinitely Demanding* by Simon Critchley.
Jen Angel on *Dream* by Stephen Duncombe.
Bryan Doherty on *A World of Gangs* by Johm Hagedorn.

SEND CHEQUES TO "UTA PUBLICATIONS"
998 BLOOR ST. WEST, P.O. BOX 10571, TORONTO ON CANADA M6H 4H9
OR ORDER ONLINE AT WWW.UPPINGTHEANTI.ORG